WITHDRAWN

AMERICAN CITIES CHRONOLOGY SERIES

CHICAGO
A CHRONOLOGICAL & DOCUMENTARY HISTORY

1784-1970

Compiled and Edited by
HOWARD B. FURER

Series Editor
HOWARD B. FURER

1974
OCEANA PUBLICATIONS, INC.
Dobbs Ferry, New York

For Cara and Keith

Library of Congress Cataloging in Publication Data

Furer, Howard B   1934-
   Chicago: a chronological and documentary history, 1784-1970.

   (American cities chronology series)
   SUMMARY: A chronological history of Chicago, its growth and development, including pertinent documents.
   Bibliography: p.
   1. Chicago--History--Chronology. 2. Chicago--History--Sources. 1. Chicago--History I. Title.
F548.3.F87   977.3'11   73-3078
ISBN 0-379-00609-X

©Copyright 1974 by Oceana Publications, Inc.

All rights reserved. No part of this publication may be reproduced or transmitted in any form or by any means, electronic or mechanical, including photocopy, recording, xerography, or any information storage and retrieval system, without permission in writing from the publisher.

Manufactured in the United States of America

TABLE OF CONTENTS

EDITOR'S FOREWORD.   v

CHRONOLOGY   1
   From Prairie Village to Booming City, 1784-1871   1
   From Holocaust to Great White City, 1872-1899 19
   The Bustling Metropolis, 1900-1939 33
   Chicago: World Metropolis, 1940-1970 51

DOCUMENTS 65
   The First Charter of the Town of Chicago, 1831 66
   The Charter of 1835. 68
   The First City Charter of Chicago, 1837. 70
   The Chicago Consolidation Act, 1851 72
   The City Charter of 1863. 74
   The Fire Department, 1863 75
   The Board of Health, 1867 77
   The Charter of 1870 79
   The Great Chicago Fire 82
   A Building Construction Ordinance, 1872. 84
   The Illinois General Charter Act, 1872 86
   Chicago Suburbs, 1873. 88
   The Haymarket Affair, 1886 89
   The Chicago Sanitary District, 1889. 92
   The World's Columbian Exposition, 1890 94
   The Pullman Strike, 1894 95
   Prostitution in Chicago, 1894. 97
   The Chicago Stockyards, 1899 98
   The Tenement House Ordinance, 1902. 99
   The Iroquois Theatre Fire, 1903 102
   The Chicago Plan Commission, 1909 106
   The Eastland Tragedy, 1915 108
   The Chicago Race Riot, 1919 111
   A Zoning Ordinance, 1923 113
   The St. Valentine's Day Massacre, 1929. 116
   A Czech Becomes Mayor, 1931 119
   The Chicago Municipal Code, 1931 121
   The Chicago World's Fair, 1933 123
   Chicago Tomorrow, 1945 126
   Mayor Daley of Chicago, 1955 128
   Shoot to Kill, Shoot to Maim, 1968 134
   The Walker Report, 1968 137

BIBLIOGRAPHY 139
   Books 139
      Articles 148

NAME INDEX 151

EDITOR'S FOREWORD

The purpose of this books is to relate in a concise form the history, growth and development of the great middle-western metropolis ---- Chicago. A detailed chronology, a series of primary documents, and interesting contemporary accounts, and an annotated bibliography form the three sections of this work. Obviously, much more could have been included in a study dealing with Chicago, but space limitations forced the author to be highly selective in his choice of materials. No single volume can possibly cover the phenomenal growth of the "Windy City," and this book does not presume to be the definitive history of this great urban complex. However, it does provide a good starting point for those persons interested in furthering their own, and our knowledge of the subject. A number of sources were utilized by the author to compile the chronology section of this volume.

Because the very nature of preparing a chronology of this type precludes the author from using the standard form of historical footnoting, I should like to acknowledge, in the editor's foreword, the major sources used to compile the bulk of the chronological and factual materials comprising the chronology section of this work. They are as follows: Emmett Dedman, Fabulous Chicago, New York, 1953; Alex Gottfried, Boss Cermak of Chicago, Seattle, 1962, and Harold M. Mayer, and Richard C. Wade, Chicago: Growth of a Metropolis, Chicago, 1969.

Howard B. Furer
Kean College of New Jersey
Union, New Jersey

CHRONOLOGY

FROM PRAIRIE VILLAGE TO BOOMING CITY, 1784-1871

1784	A black furtrapper, Jean Baptiste Point du Sable, was the first settler in what is now Chicago.
1803	Fort Dearborn, on the Chicago River, was established. The city of Chicago would be built on this site.
1814	Fort Dearborn was destroyed, and its population wiped out by Indian attacks.
1816	A second Fort Dearborn was constructed.
1827	The Illinois State Legislature obtained a Federal land grant to help finance a waterway from Lake Michigan to the Chicago River to the Desplaines River, and into the Mississippi River. This canal was the most important factor in the founding and early growth of Chicago.
1829	Archibald Clybourne built the first meat packing plant in the town.
1832	The population of the town stood at about one hundred people.

Cholera broke out in Chicago, forcing some of the inhabitants to move into the surrounding countryside.

The first lighthouse in Chicago was built.

March. John Watkins, the first school teacher in the town arrived.

April 25. The first street in Chicago was surveyed. It ran from the east end of Water Street to Lake Michigan.

August 4. James Thompson filed the first survey of the town. Chicago received its first legal geographical location.

October. Town lots in Chicago were selling for $35. |
| 1833 | August 12. The village of Chicago was organized with a population of a little more than four hundred people. Its first charter provided for an area of one square mile.

The "balloon frame style" of building construction was developed by Augustine Deodat Taylor, who built St. Mary's Church in the fledgling town.

The first printing office in Chicago was begun. |

The first lumber mill in Chicago was erected.

September. Eliza Chappel opened Chicago's first public school.

September 26. Seventy-six Indian chiefs signed a treaty, giving up their lands at Chicago, and in the surrounding vicinity. They left the area in 1835.

November 26. The Chicago Democrat, the first newspaper in Chicago was published.

1834

John H. Kinzie was appointed the first President of the Village of Chicago.

Town lots sold for $3,500 each, as real-estate values began to rise rapidly.

As a result of land speculation, Chicago's population grew to 1,800 people.

The channel at the mouth of the Chicago River was enlarged, thereby improving the water access to the town.

The first music school in Chicago was organized.

The Dearborn Street Drawbridge, connecting the settlements on either side of the river was erected. It was the first bridge across the Chicago River.

January 1. A mail route from Chicago to Ottawa, Illinois was opened.

July. The first ship to enter the Port of Chicago was the one hundred ton schooner, Illinois.

November. As late as November, there were only two girls of marriageable age in Chicago.

1835

The first Chicago pier on Lake Michigan was built.

Chicago's first hotel was the Lake House, built of brick, at the corner of Rush and North Water Streets.

January. The Federal Land Office in Chicago began the sale, by auction, of government lots along the route of the proposed canal between Lake Michigan and the Mississippi River. The canal helped to cause a land boom in the town between 1835 and 1837.

February 11. The Town of Chicago was incorporated with a population of 3,456 people.

October. The first court house and jail in Chicago was built at the corner of Clark and Randolph Streets.

1836

The Henry B. Clarke House, Chicago's first so-called "suburban" dwelling was built.

The first lawyer to come to Chicago, Russell E. Heacock, arrived from New England.

"Long John" Wentworth arrived in Chicago. He soon became one of the leading citizens of the town.

January. A second public auction of lots along the canal route sold 186 plots in the Chicago vicinity.

1837

March 4. Chicago, with a population of 4,170 people, was incorporated as a city, receiving its first city charter from the Illinois State Legislature.

April. William B. Ogden, who came from New York, was elected Chicago's first mayor

A city ordinance was passed stating that only those owning a "freehold estate" were eligible for the major elective posts in the city. In addition, in order to vote, Chicagoans had to be householders, or were required to pay a city tax of not less than three dollars per year.

Advances in land values in Chicago of twenty and twenty-five percent per day were not unusual by this date.

May. The City Council passed an ordinance prohibiting the construction of buildings in the area east of Michigan Avenue from Randolph Street to Park Row. Although the ordinance specifically stated "forever," it was soon repeatedly violated.

June. The first theater in Chicago was opened in the dining room of the Sauganash Hotel.

There were already seventeen lawyers' offices in the city.

September. Although the panic of 1837 struck hard in Chicago, by September, the city had rebounded, and its reputation as a commercially sound community began to spread.

1838 Robert Fergus opened a printing establishment in the city.

The first thirty-eight bags of wheat were shipped east from Chicago.

Built on land about two feet above the lake level, the city made an attempt to escape the mud by laying wooden planks across the streets.

1839 Chicago's newspaper, the <u>Daily American</u> was founded by William Stuart.

April. William Ogden was reelected mayor.

October 27. A large fire destroyed buildings on both Dearborn and Lake Streets.

1840 The population of Chicago was 4,470.

The effects of the panic of 1837 were still being felt in Chicago. Real estate values dropped, prices fell, and debts mounted. Land bought for $11,000 and acre in 1836, could not be sold for $100 in 1840.

The Irish began settling in Chicago in an area known as "Back of the Yards."

Chicagoans openly expressed their resentment over the fact that their mayor was paid a salary.

February. The first official hanging in the city took place at what is now Twenty-Ninth Street and South Parkway. The second public execution did not take place until seventeen years later.

1841 The City Council granted a license to the managers of the Sauganash Hotel Theater to maove their operations to a building nearer the business district. The leading players of this new theater were Mr. & Mrs. Joseph Jefferson.

CHRONOLOGY 5

Two hundred and twelve bushels of wheat were shipped east from Chicago.

April. Buckner S. Morris was elected mayor.

1842 Some 586,907 bushels of wheat were shipped east from Chicago. This fantastic increase showed signs of the city's rapid commercial growth.

The Second Presbyterian Church of Chicago was established.

The oldest German singing society in the United States, the Sacred Music Society, was organized.

1843 April. August Garrett was elected mayor.

1844 Tonnage entering and clearing the Port of Chicago reached 440,000 tons.

By this year, meat packing became important among the businesses of Chicago.

May 10. John Quarter was consecrated the first Catholic Bishop of Chicago, by Arch-Bishop John Hughes of New York who came to the city for the ceremony.

1845 September 1. Chicago's first permanent school building was erected, mainly through the efforts of Ira Miltimore, a prominent citizen. This was the Dearborn School on Madison Street between Dearborn and State Streets.

1846 February 5. A group of Chicago citizens, headed by William Ogden, bought the charter and the land for the construction of a railroad between Chicago and Galena, Illinois.

1847 The first Chicago theater of note was built by John B. Rice on the southside of Randolph Street. It was here that opera was first presented in the city. However, the theater burned down during the first performance.

March. Three brothers from Rockbridge County, Virginia, began the development, in Chicago, of a farm machinery business. They were the McCormick brothers, the eldest of which was Cyrus who invented the reaper. By 1850, Cyrus had built the business into a world-wide enterprise, and had become a millionaire.

May. The first convention, but certainly not the last, was held in Chicago. It was the River and Harbor Convention, attended by three thousand delegates from Eastern and Western States, who were complaining about Federal neglect of internal improvements in their regions. This massive protest meeting included many prominent Americans, including Horace Greeley, Tom Corwin, Erastus Corning, and Abraham Lincoln.

June 10. The <u>Chicago Tribune</u> began publication.

1848   January. The Chicago Board of Trade was created.

February 17. The <u>Illinois-Staats-Zeitung</u> began publication in Chicago. It was one of more than thirty German periodicals published in the city at one time or another, as Chicago became one of the favorite places for the settlement of the hordes of German immigrants coming to the United States in the nineteenth century.

March. As of this date, Chicago did not have a single mile of railroad track. Within six years time, the city became the railroad center of the West.

April. The Illinois and Michigan Canal was opened after twelve years of construction. The farms of the interior now used Chicago as their primary market.

November 20. The Chicago and Calena Union Railroad opened for business, beginning Chicago's railroad career.

1849   Three markets were established in the city for the retailing of perishable foods.

By 1849, Chicago already had more gambling establishments than Philadelphia or Boston.

September. Adolph Mueller, a German immigrant, began to brew Chicago's first beer.

1850   The population of Chicago reached 29,963.

Beginning in 1850, an army of travelling salesmen (drummers) began setting out from Chicago to sell a long list of Chicago wares to shopkeepers in small towns across the country.

Fredrika Bremer, the famous Swedish novelist visited Chicago, and called it the most miserable and ugly city in America.

Large groups of Swedes and Norwegians began to arrive in the city. Some remained, but the majority moved on to farms in the interior.

G.P.A. Healy, the noted portrait painter arrived in the city, and became a permanent resident.

A group of young men met to outline plans for a mid-west university in Chicago, which would help create a "community of desirable citizens." Its leaders were Grant Goodrich, John Evans, and Orrington Lunt.

February. The Chicago Philharmonic Society was founded. However, it was disbanded two years later.

April. Julius Dyhrenfurth conducted a twenty-two man orchestra in a symphony concert to dedicate the music hall at the Tremont House Hotel.

Chicago's first omnibus line was opened. It ran from downtown to what is now Lincoln Park.

June. Chicago's entrepreneurs eager to have railroad depots built, sold to the Illinois Central Railroad, at a token price, the site of the old fort Dearborn on the lake shore.

1851

The Illinois Central Railroad was chartered. It was the first land grant railroad in the United States.

Allan Pinkerton was hired as Chicago's first detective.

January 28. Northwestern University, originally a Methodist College, was founded in what was to become the Evanston suburb of Chicago.

Chicago became the largest corn market in the United States, and by 1854, it was the largest wheat market in the nation.

February 1. The Chicago Consolidation Act went into effect. It explained rather than increased the powers of the city government.

March. By an act of the City Council, butchers in Chicago were permitted to open meat markets outside of the three central markets.

April. The mayor of Chicago was given a veto power over acts passed by the City Council.

The City Council passed an ordinance providing for the planting of trees along the streets and in the public grounds of the city.

1852

The Michigan Southern and Michigan Central Railroad lines entered Chicago from the east.

In order to save the city the expense of building a breakwater along the lake, the city government turned over to the Illinois Central Railroad, the entire lake shore to the city's southern edge.

April. All property requirements for voting and officeholding were removed by the City Council.

1853

Primarily as a result of railroad building, Chicago's population increased to well over sixty thousand people.

By 1853, Chicago had seven daily newspapers.

John B. Rice constructed another theater, in which he presented a full season of Italian opera.

The Court House, designed by Chicago's first important architect, John M. Van Osdel, was built.

The first two stories of the Galena and Chicago Union Railroad depot were constructed. A third story was added in 1863, and this station remained in operation until 1911. The present day Merchandise Mart stands on its site.

Evanston, the largest, and one of the oldest suburbs of Chicago was incorporated.

April. Thomas Dyer was elected mayor.

1854

Chicago's first publicly owned Water Works, located at Lake Michigan and Chicago Avenues, was completed.

The first issue of the Chicago Times was published. It lasted until 1895.

Chicago established a paid, municipal fire-fighting department.

February 22. The Chicago and Rock Island completed its line from the city to the town of Rock Island, Illinois on the Mississippi River. Henry Farnam and Joseph Sheffield were the chief engineers in charge of building the road.

May 30. The passage of the Kansas-Nebraska Act was extremely unpopular among Chicagoans who voiced their opposition to the measure in a number of public demonstrations.

September 1. Stephen A. Douglas, Senator from Illinois, and the sponsor of the Kansas-Nebraska Act, spoke to a crowd of ten thousand at Market Hall, where he defended the passage of the measure. He was booed repeatedly, and was prevented from addressing the crowd further.

1855

The Illinois Central freight shed was erected. It still stands today.

Ellis S. Chesbrough was appointed Chief Engineer of the Board of Sewerage Commissioners of Chicago.

The city government began the job of raising the level of the streets twelve feet, and filling in twelve hundred acres of swamp land in and around the city.

By 1855, Chicago had ten trunk lines, eleven branch lines, and ninety-six trains were entering the city each day.

Three bookstores existed in the city, one of which was the largest in the Mid-west.

The world famous singer Adelina Patti gave a concert in the city. At the same performance, the great Norwegian violinist, Ole Bull also appeared.

Chicago's death rate exceeded that of New Orleans, as a result of yearly epidemics of typhoid, smallpox, and cholera. Tuberculosis in the city was also quite bad.

The Western Union Telegraph lines were opened from Chicago to New Orleans, thereby linking the South and the Middle-West.

January. Franklin Parmalee began the omnibus company known as the "Citizens Line."

April. Dr. Levi D. Boone was elected mayor. He was the candidate of the "Know-Nothing" party which had great popularity in Chicago during the 1850's.

April 21. A riot broke out among police and Chicago saloon keepers, aided by scores of immigrants, as a result of Mayor Boone's attempt to stop the drinking of beer in the city, which he regarded as "foreign and un-American."

1856

The Marine Bank Building at the corner of La Salle and Lake Streets was constructed.

The Illinois Central Railroad, linking Chicago, Galena, and Cairo, Illinois was completed. This road brought into Chicago markets, downstate produce that would have otherwise gone to St. Louis. Chicagoans called the road "the St. Louis cut-off." The great Chicago-St. Louis rivalry began as a result of this railroad construction.

Eighteen omnibus lines were making more than four hundred trips daily.

Lake Forest began to be developed as Chicago's most exclusive suburb.

The Chicago Historical Society was organized. It had a collection of eleven thousand books and began accumulating maps and manuscripts.

March. The initial horsecar railroads were enfranchised.

July. Two schooners, the <u>Dean Richmond</u> and the <u>Madeira Pet</u>, carried the first cargoes of wheat from Chicago through the canals, around the St. Lawrence rapids, and across the Atlantic to Liverpool. These voyages inaugurated direct trade with overseas countries, and established Chicago as an international port.

1857

The North Chicago Rolling Mill was established on the west bank of the North Branch of the Chicago River. Blast furnaces were added in 1870, and a Bessemer Converter in 1872.

The first Nicholson pavement was laid in Chicago.

The Chicago SouthBranchCanal, which entered the lumber yards, was completed.

The original Fort Dearborn was demolished.

The Chicago Relief and Aid Society was incorporated.

The Chicago United Charities was established.

By 1857, the city had acquired alternate water and rail connections with New York, when the New York Central Railroad entered the city.

The State Street Market Hall, Chicago's second public market, was constructed with public funds on State Street.

March. George P. Upton started the Mendelssohn Society, which later became the Apollo Club.

April. After serving several terms in Congress, "Long" John Wentworth was elected mayor.

April 20. Mayor Wentworth, with the help of Chicago's fire department destroyed an area in the North Side along the lake front known as "The Sands," which was notorious for its saloons, gambling dens, and bordellos.

June 18. Mayor Wentworth ordered the police to remove every overhanging sign, awning, and all posts or other obstructions from the downtown streets that had been blocking the sidewalks.

1858

Henry Fuller, Franklin Parmalee, and Liberty Bigelow began building the first horsecar line in the City. These lines ran until 1900.

Abraham Lincoln began his campaign for the Senate by making a speech from the balcony of the Tremont House Hotel in Chicago.

There were more than one hundred houses of prostitution in the city by 1858.

By 1858, Chicago was the chief grain shipper of the United

States, with some twenty million bushels being sent out of the city annually.

January 1. Chicago policemen were required to wear uniforms for the first time in the city's history.

February. Mayor Wentworth reorganized the municipal fire department, and brought the first steam fire engine into the city.

April. George Pullman raised the Tremont House, the largest hotel in the city, eight feet, using the efforts of twelve hundred men and the power of five thousand jackscrews. Like the raising of the sidewalks, this was undertaken to alleviate the drainage and mud problem.

September. Abraham Lincoln debated Stephen A. Douglas on the balcony of the Tremont House on the question of slavery and popular sovereignty. Lincoln won the debate, but Douglas received the large Democratic vote in Chicago, and was sent back to the Senate.

1859   The first horse drawn railway line in the city went into operation.

The armoured truck company, Brinks Incorporated, was founded in Chicago.

General George B. McClellan established the Kenwood Station of the Illinois Central Railroad when he was vice-president of the company.

The first University of Chicago opened. In June, 1886, due to a lack of funds and internal problems it closed.

April. John Wentworth was re-elected mayor.

1860   Chicago's population reached 109,620 people. Fifty percent of the population was foreign born.

By 1860, Chicago became the center of the world's largest rail network.

To attract the Republican National Convention of 1860, Chicago businessmen paid for the construction of the Wigwam Building at Lake and Market Streets. The building was only a huge hall. It was built in five weeks, and provided the setting for the nomination of Abraham Lincoln.

The Chicago Zouaves, a company of military cadets, organized by Colonel Elmer Ellsworth, toured the East, taking part in a series of precision drill contests. Ellsworth was the first Union officer to fall in the Civil War.

January. Mayor Wentworth, in order to cut costs, reduced the size of the police force to fifty-seven officers and men, hardly enough to police Chicago with a population of more than 109,000.

April. The Illinois State Legislature set up an independent police board for Chicago, which took control of the police function out of the mayor's hands.

June. Mayor Wentworth went to Montreal to invite Albert Edward (later Edward VII) to visit Chicago, which he did the following month.

November 6. In the presidential election, most Chicagoans voted for Stephen A. Douglas and the Democrats, although a large percentage of the city's foreign born, especially the Germans, cast their ballots for the Republicans and Abraham Lincoln.

1861   The closing of the Mississippi River to Northern trade as a result of the Civil War, was a boon to the east-west railroads, benefiting Chicago.

The Chicago Police Department was given the responsibility, by the City Council, of caring for the city's health.

April. John C. Haines was elected mayor.

April 12. From the beginning of the Civil War, Chicago experienced a business boom as speculators in war goods swarmed into the city.

April 20. The city's four hundred member militia were ordered to Cairo, Illinois to guard the Ohio and Mississippi Rivers.

June. Chicago's "Irish Regiment" was sent to Lexington, Missouri, where it fought bravely, but was forced to surrender to the Confederate forces.

1863 The Chicago Erring Women's Refuge For Reform opened its doors.

By 1863, Chicago had displaced Cincinnati as the pork-packing center of the United States.

A Soldier's Fair was held in the city to raise money for the Sanitary Commission.

Camp Douglas in Chicago was converted into a prisoner of war camp for Confederate troops captured at Fort Donelson.

January. Wilbur F. Storey, editor of the <u>Chicago Times</u>, who had originally supported the Northern cause in the Civil War, suddenly became its most vehement opponent in Chicago.

February 13. The city received a new charter, granting the municipality additional powers.

February 20. General J. B. Sweet, stationed in Chicago, was ordered to censure Storey and the <u>Times</u>. This action caused a riot, and President Lincoln revoked the order.

1864 The city's patriotic song writer, George F. Root, composed a series of war ballads, including "The Battle Cry of Freedom," and "Tramp, Tramp, Tramp."

George M. Pullman built the "Pioneer," the first especially constructed sleeping car in Chicago. Three years later, he organized the Pullman Palace Car Company in the city.

The <u>Working Man's Advocate</u>, an anti-capitalist newspaper, and one of the most influential labor papers in the country, began to be published in Chicago.

Samuel J. Walker developed Ashland Boulevard between Monroe and Harrison Streets by widening the streets, planting trees, installing sewers and pavement, and constructing six expensive houses at different corners.

Union Park was opened to the public.

February. The Chicago Typographical Union went on strike against Chicago newspapers.

CHRONOLOGY 15

August. The so-called "Chicago Conspiracy," a plot to free Confederate prisoners by secret organizations in the city sympathetic toward the South, was temporarily abandoned.

August 29. The Democratic National Convention was held in a specially constructed amphitheater in Chicago.

November. The "Chicago Conspiracy" was uncovered, arrests were made, and the plot was brought to an end.

1865

By 1865, Clark and Lake Streets had become the center of Chicago. Land values reached $2,000 a foot in that area.

The first Chamber of Commerce Building on Court House Square was completed.

The North Chicago Rolling Mills produced the first steel rails in America.

The Chicago Academy of Music (later the Chicago Musical College, 1867) was founded.

The dry goods and household furnishing store of Field, Leiter and Company opened.

January. The Crosby Opera House was opened by its foun founder, Uranus H. Crosby.

March. Another Soldier's Fair was held to raise funds for returning veterans. It was much more elaborate than the one held two years earlier.

April. John B. Rice was elected mayor.

May 1. President Lincoln's funeral procession arrived in Chicago, where the body lay in state at the Court House for a day and night.

December 25. The Union Stockyards were opened. They were built with community effort.

1866

A cholera epidemic broke out in Chicago, brought to the city by a Mormon immigrant. - FIGURES.

Funds raised through thousands of pledges were used to

erect a monument to Stephen A. Douglas, who had died in 1861. It still stands on the lake shore near Thirty-fifth Street.

Construction began on Lincoln Park, which was part of the general plan to create a ring of parks around the city.

The Upper Arch of the Water Tunnel was constructed. By 1880, a second tunnel was installed leading to the West Side Pumping Works at Blue Island and Ashland Avenues.

1867

Potter Palmer was the first millionaire of Chicago, having made his fortune in cotton speculation during the Civil War. He was also one of the city's great realtors, and in 1867, he bought three-quarters of a mile of land along State Street.

The first LaSalle Street Station was completed at a cost of $225,000. Six hundred and fourteen million feet of lumber were sold in Chicago during the year, making her the largest lumber market in the world.

The city government began the construction of a new waterworks by pumping water through a two mile tunnel under Lake Michigan.

The "crib," an octagonal box of about fifty feet in diameter, and seventy feet long was sunk in about forty feet of water in Lake Michigan. The two mile tunnel under the lake was connected with the "crib," thereby comprising the most important section of Chicago's new waterworks system.

January. Philip D. Armour opened a meat-packing plant in Chicago.

March 9. The Illinois State Legislature allowed the city of Chicago to set up a Board of Health.

March 25. The Chicago Water Tower's cornerstone was laid. The Tower, a Gothic structure, eventually rose to a height of one hundred and thirty feet. It's architect was William W. Boyington. By 1869, the Tower was nearly completed.

April. John B. Rice was re-elected mayor.

1868

The Pioneer Park Zoo opened in the city.

The city held its first charity-society ball at Crosby's Opera House. It had been suggested by P.G. Gilmore, a band leader, who became one of the leading musical figures of the city.

A great fire on Lake Street caused more than two million dollars worth of damage. A new business district began to develop on State Street.

One of America's first Polish churches, St. Stanislaus Kostka was begun.

May 20-21. Ulysses S. Grant was nominated for the presidency at the Republican National Convention, which met at Crosby's Opera House.

July. The City Council passed an ordinance limiting the amount of time a bridge across the river could be opened to ten minutes, so as to facilitate better transit from one side of the river to the other, and to avoid traffic jams.

1869

Refrigerator cars were developed. They proved a boon to meat-packers in Chicago.

The Hannibal and St. Joseph Railroad rached Chicago, linking the big cattle town of Kansas City with the stockyards of the city.

Chicago's first finance company was established.

Theodore Thomas and his orchestra played a series of concerts in Chicago.

The Norwood Park section of the city was laid out by the Norwood Park Land Building Association.

The merchants of Chicago, unable to control the operations of grain warehousemen through the Chicago Board of Trade, demanded a provision in the State Constitution of 1869 authorizing the regulation of warehouses. The State Legislature took prompt action the following year.

Tonnage entering and clearing the Port of Chicago reached well over three million tons.

The West Side Park System was laid out.

January. The Washington Street Tunnel, under the South Branch of the Chicago River, was completed. It connected the West Side with downtown.

May 10. The completion of the Union Pacific Railroad, the first transcontinental, gave Chicago a direct line to San Francisco. In fact, by the 1880's, Chicago was the eastern terminus for all the great transcontinental lines.

November. Burlesque was first presented in the United States at Crosby's Opera House by Lydia Thompson and her "British Blondes."

1870

The population of Chicago increased to 299,000 people. Nearly 145,000 of these inhabitants were foreign-born.

The Society For the Promotion of Social Purity was formed to "help the fallen" and to study the causes of prostitution.

The Chicago Board of Trade began the inspection and grading of meat at the stockyards.

By 1870, Chicago was the leading meat packer, and the leading grain and lumber market in the United States.

April. A new charter for Chicago was adopted by the voters. It gave the city new and greater powers.

September 26. The two hundred and twenty-five room hotel, the Palmer House, built for two hundred thousand dollars by the architect John M. Van Osdel, was opened.

1871

More than three hundred thousand people lived within the boundaries of Chicago, which were six miles long from north to south, and three miles wide.

In 1871, Chicago's total grain elevator storage was 11,375,000 bushels.

Twenty one main line railroad tracks entered the city by this date.

The Water Tank Library was established in an abandoned water tank near the river.

January. The Chicago Board of Trade sponsored a Warehousing Act, which was passed to control practices in grain warehousing in the city.

April. Roswell B. Mason was elected mayor.

June. Chicago began a large engineering project, headed by Ellis S. Chesbrough, to change the direction of the Chicago River, into which the city's sewers emptied, so that it flowed into the Illinois River, rather than Lake Michigan. The project had little effect.

July. The LaSalle Street Tunnel was opened.

October 8-9. The great Chicago fire raged throughout certain sections of the city. It began in a barn owned by Mrs. Kate O'Leary of DeKoven Street. The blaze continued for two days, destroying millions of dollars worth of property, and leaving one hundred thousand people homeless. New construction, however, began immediately after the fire was put out.

October 17. The Young Men's Christian Association of Chicago was begun at a public meeting. In 1873, its name was changed to the Chicago Athenaeum.

FROM HOLOCAUST TO GREAT WHITE CITY, 1872-1899

1872

A new law requiring two-thirds rather than a majority of the elected Councilmen, to override the Mayor's veto, was passed.

The city tried twice to establish reform groups, once with a Committee of Seventy, and again with a Committee of Twenty-five. Both groups broke up in fights.

A so-called Bread Riot took place in front of the offices of the Relief and Aid Society on LaSalle Street.

The City Council passed an ordinance outlawing wooden buildings in the downtown area.

The Inter-State Industrial Exposition Building was erected. It stood until 1892, when it was torn down to make room for the Art Institute.

The three hundred room Sherman House Hotel was built.

The State of Illinois enacted legislation to control City Council appropriations in Chicago, as a result of the city's inability to pay its debts.

The mail order house of Montgomery Ward and Company opened in Chicago.

March. New city ordinances were passed, which stated that only brick or stone buildings could be erected in the city's business district.

May. Construction began on the second Chamber of Commerce Building.

1873　　Queen Victoria sent a contribution to the City of Chicago to be used for the construction of a new public library.

Chicago experienced another large fire that did considerable damage.

The new Grand Pacific Hotel was erected.

George Pullman commissioned John M. Dunphy, a Chicago architect to build a mansion at 1729 Prairie Avenue.

A new Field and Leiter Store was built, but like the first one, it too was destroyed by fire. A third one was built in 1878.

February. The McCormick works moved to a new twenty-four acre site at Blue Island and Western Avenues on the South Branch of the Chicago River.

September. An Inter-State Industrial Exposition was held in the city to show the progress Chicago had made following its great fire.

September 18. When the panic of 1873 struck, Chicago was able to weather the storm fairly well, partly because of a backlog of funds that had been donated by rival cities to help out after the destruction done by the great fire in 1871. In addition, Chicago banks refused to close their doors.

November. Joseph Medill, by campaigning on the issue of

fire prevention, was elected mayor.

1874   A number of reform associations appeared in 1874 under various names. One of the most important leaders of these groups was Franklin MacVeah, who urged the city government to assume all municipal affairs.

A Committee of One Hundred was formed to clean up the city's graft and corruption. It failed to accomplish anything.

Melville E. Stone began the publication of the <u>Chicago Daily News</u>.

March. The first suburban train of the Chicago and Northwestern Railway began operating between the city and Park Ridge.

June. A Society For the Suppression of Vice was organized.

September. Lake View High School was opened after the State Legislature passed a law allowing townships to establish high schools.

1875   By 1875, more steel rails were made in Chicago than in any other American city.

The headquarters of Armour and Company were moved from Milwaukee to Chicago.

The new Palmer House Hotel was constructed by Van Osdel.

Augustus Swift arrived in Chicago and established his meatpacking house.

By 1875, Chicago had nearly one hundred suburbs with a total population of fifty thousand, located along the railroads running out of the city.

Chicago showed no signs of the great fire of four years earlier, as the city had been completely rebuilt.

January. The <u>Chicago Daily News</u> was becoming the city's largest newspaper. By 1881, it had a circulation of fifty thousand and by 1890, one of one hundred and thirty thousand. On its staff were such writers and reporters as George Harvey, Henry Guy Carelton, James Whitcomb Riley, and

Finley Peter Dunne.

April. Chicago voters adopted the Illinois General City Charter Law of 1872, which established the general framework of Chicago's city government. With minor amendments, it is still basically in operation today.

Henry D. Colvin was elected mayor.

1876   The Chicago Citizen's Law and Order League was formed to enforce laws prohibiting the sale of liquor to minors.

Two years after Augustus Swift arrived in Chicago, his packing company began shipping meat to the East.

Despite its rapid growth, as late as 1877, Chicago still contained thirty thousand vaults and cesspools.

April. Monroe Heath was elected mayor.

July 17. A railroad worker's strike, begun in Baltimore, spread to Chicago, paralyzing every railroad yard in the city. Lumbermen and other workers also struck in sympathy. A number of people were killed before the strike ended.

December. The Chicago Commercial Club was founded.

1878   The first modern apartment building in Chicago was constructed on Erie Street.

The first telephone exchange in the city was established.

1879   The Chicago Art Institute was organized. Its first building on Michigan Avenue was completed in 1882.

April. Carter H. Harrison was elected mayor. He was one of the city's most popular chief executives, known as "our Carter."

1880   Chicago's population reached more than five hundred thousand.

By 1880, Chicago was the greatest interior city in America. It had surpassed its chief rival St. Louis, and had fifteen thousand miles of railroads, connecting it with all of the areas of the upper Mississippi Valley and the Northwest.

A citizen's association, whose purpose was to control land use in residential areas, was organized.

The magazine, the Dial, was founded in Chicago by Francis F. Browne. It dealt with critical literary appraisals.

The first building inspection powers in the city were granted to the Health and Building Departments.

1881 The Chicago and Northwestern Depot at Wells and Kinzie Streets was erected. It was used until 1911, when it was replaced by the present terminal on West Madison Street.

Chemical fire engines were introduced in the city.

The Montauk Block Building designed by Daniel Burnham, and John W. Root was built. Its "floating raft" foundation solved the problem of how to build large structures on the soft under-soil of the area.

Marshall Field and Company, Chicago's biggest retail store, opened under the sole ownership of Marshall Field, who had bought out all the other interests in the concern. Field made several pioneering innovations in retail merchandising.

Louis Sullivan, the noted architect, formed a partnership with Dankmar Adler. It lasted until 1900, and produced some notable works in the city.

April. Carter H. Harrison was re-elected mayor.

1882 The Chicago professional baseball team opened a new ball park, and erected the first large grandstand in the United States.

Traffic on the Illinois-Michigan Canal reached its height, but after 1882, declined.

The Chicago Stock Exchange was established.

January. Charles T. Yerkes built the first cable car line in the city. Chicago's cable car not only climbed hills, but also turned corners.

1883 — George Pullman and Marshall Field were influential forces in the Commercial Club's sponsorship of the Chicago Manual Training School founded in 1883.

The Confederate prison, Libby Prison in Virginia, was brought to Chicago, stone by stone, and rebuilt as a museum in 1883.

April. Carter H. Harrison was re-elected for a third term.

1884 — The Home Insurance Building was constructed. It was the first tall building, embodying the basic principles of iron frame design. It was planned by William LeBaron Jenney, and stood at the corner of La Salle and Adams Streets until it was torn down in 1930.

The Chicago Conservatory of Music was established.

June 3. The Republican National Convention met in Chicago.

July 8. The Democratic National Convention met in Chicago.

1885 — The Chicago Motor Club Building was erected. It was demolished in 1929 to make way for the Chicago Club Building.

Forty thousand persons paid admission to a four game series between the Chicago White Sox and the New York Metropolitans at the Chicago Club Grounds.

John Van Osdel's City Hall and County Building was completed.

By 1885, the Chicago River had thirty-five movable bridges across it, and two tunnels under it. Despite this, serious congestion continued across the river from one part of the city to the other.

The twelve story Rookery Building, designed by Burnham and Root, was erected.

April. Carter H. Harrison was re-elected mayor for an unprecedented fourth term.

1886 — Sears, Roebuck and Company was established in Chicago.

The Chicago City Council set aside small areas in its public parks for playing fields.

The Chicago Symphony Orchestra, conducted by Hans Balatka, was organized.

March. A strike was called at the McCormick works in Chicago, and picket lines were formed along the so-called Black Road.

April. Chicago police, attempting to break up a meeting of workers along Black Road, fired into the crowd, killing six men.

May 1. An eight-hour-day general strike was begun in the city among all labor groups.

May 4. The Haymarket Massacre occurred in Chicago, when, after police broke up an Anarcho-Communist meeting at Haymarket Square, a bomb exploded among the police, who then opened fire on the crowd. Seven policemen were killed, and seventy people were wounded.

June 19-August 20. The trial of August Spies, Albert Parsons, and Samuel F. Fielden, and other radical agitators at the Haymarket Massacre, before Judge Joseph E. Gary in Chicago, resulted in convictions. Seven men were sentenced to death, and one to fifteen years in prison.

1887

The first building erected completely of wrought-iron skeleton construction was the thirteen story Tacoma Building in Chicago.

Chicago was designated a central reserve city.

The Outer Belt Line (Elgin, Joliet and Eastern Railroad) was completed. It helped the outward spread of Chicago by the development of suburban communities such as Chicago Heights.

A packinghouse lockout occurred in Chicago causing more labor unrest.

March 3. Fort Sheridan was built along the lake front. It was manned by Army troops to reassure Chicagoans that their property would not be subject to destruction by anarchists such as the Haymarket group.

November 11. Four of the convicted Haymarket "bombers" were executed in Chicago.

1888   "Pop" A.C. Anson's Chicago White Sox played a series of exhibition games around the world.

A campaign to make libraries centers of adult education was begun in the city.

1889   Ellen Gates Starr and Jane Addams founded Hull House in Chicago, a settlement house devoted to the improvement of the city's slums. It was the prototype of all others established in the United States.

The Leiter Building, using William Le Baron Jenney's new type of building construction, was erected.

C.J. Van Depoele began the first electric railway system (trolley car) in the city.

The Chicago Auditorium was erected. The major force behind its construction was Ferdinand Wythe Peck. The opera star Adelina Patti "opened" the hall.

John Crerar gave $2,500,000 for the founding of a library in the city that bears his name.

Beginning in 1889, a great exodus of Chicagoans to the suburbs took place.

The City of Chicago annexed the Village of Hyde Park. Since the Town of Pullman lay within Hyde Park's boundaries, Chicago's control was now extended over the experimental town of Pullman.

The Chicago Sanitary District was established by the Illinois State Legislature. It was designed to provide for the disposal of sewage.

June 29. Chicago annexed the towns of Ravenswood and Lake View. In fact, on this day, voters in a surrounding one hundred and twenty square miles elected to join the City of Chicago.

CHRONOLOGY

1890

The population of Chicago was a little more than one million people. The city's foreign born population numbered nearly as many as its entire population in 1880, while almost seventy-eight percent of Chicago's residents were foreign born or children of foreign born.

The number of American born immigrant children in the city nearly equaled that of the total alien born.

More than seventy thousand Scandinavians were working and living in Chicago. They made up fifteen percent of the city's foreign born population.

The Negro population of Chicago was less than fifteen thousand.

By 1890, sixty-five thousand workers in Chicago were reported to be organized in labor unions, one third of them in the American Federation of Labor.

In 1890, Chicago was the most Catholic of all American cities.

John D. Rockefeller gave a large sum of money to found the Baptist Seminary in Chicago.

Chicago had 2,048 miles of streets, of which only six hundred and twenty-nine were paved, about half with woodblock, the rest with macadam, gravel, stoneblock, asphalt, cinders or cobblestones.

April 25. The United States Congress selected Chicago as the site of the World's Columbian Exposition.

June. The South Side Rapid Transit Company began construction of an elevated railway line using steam locomotives.

September. The Central Manufacturing District was organized. It was a kind of industrial park established by the Chicago Junction Railway, and the Union Stock Yards Companies.

1891

The use of medical inspectors for an annual check of all school children in Chicago began.

The twenty-one story Masonic Temple was constructed by Daniel Burnham.

Florence Kelley, a leader in the settlement house movement, came to Chicago.

The typhoid death rate reached one hundred and seventy-four per one hundred thousand people.

The Monadnock Building was completed. It was among the finest expressions of the Chicago school of architecture.

The Fair Store, originally established in 1875, was replaced by a new building on Adams Street. In 1965, it was remodeled as the downtown store of Montgomery Ward.

Samuel Insull came to Chicago. He began building a financial empire, which in 1928 was valued at four billion dollars.

January. Chicago citizens chose a site on the lake shore for the construction of the World's Columbian Exposition, while a group of architects, including Frederick L. Olmsted, Robert M. Hunt, Charles McKim, George B. Post, and Louis Sullivan, met in Chicago to plan the buildings of this great fair.

April. Carter H. Harrison was elected mayor for a fifth time.

October 16. Theodore Thomas conducted the first concert of the new Chicago Symphony Orchestra, which he had organized in 1891.

1892

The Newberry Library was built by Henry Ives Cobb. Today, it is one of the nation's major research libraries.

Telephone communications were begun between Chicago, New York and Boston.

Several new lines were added to the city's elevated railroad system.

Central Station of the Illinois-Central Railroad at Park Row was completed. It still stands today as one of the city's great terminals.

March. Congress authorized an investigation of Chicago's slums.

May. The Chicago Sanitary Commission began the project known as the Sanitary and Ship Canal, whose purpose was the building of a new route between the Mississippi River and the Great Lakes.

July. The Congress Hotel was erected.

October 1. The new University of Chicago opened. This institution was made possible by gifts of $2,600,000 donated by John D. Rockefeller. William Rainey Harper was appointed its first President.

1893

There were ten thousand prostitutes in the city, with most of the brothels located in the district between Clark and Dearborn Streets, and Harrison and Polk Streets.

The Hull House Men's Club was organized.

By 1893, the total area of Chicago was one hundred and eighty-five square miles.

Julius Rosenwald, a clothing manufacturer, bought a half interest in Sears, Roebuck and Company, By 1910, he was the firm's president, and became the richest man in Chicago. He gave away more than $63,000,000 in philanthropic projects.

There were more than five hundred miles of trolley track in the city. The trolleys carried some two hundred million fares a year.

The Chicago Natural History Museum was founded through the gifts of Marshall Field and others.

The Chicago Art Institute moved from Michigan Avenue to the lake front.

The Chicago Civic Federation was organized with Lyman J. Gage as its President. Other members of the Federation were Mrs. Potter Palmer, Marshall Field, and Cyrus McCormick Jr. Its purpose was to reform Chicago's governmental operations. Ralph M. Easley, Graham Taylor, Julia Lathrop, and Jane Addams were among its leaders.

After 1893, Chicago's Gold Coast on the Near North Side, became the residential area of the city's wealthiest families.

Chicago, by 1893, contained the third largest Bohemian community in the world.

Marshall Field's department store installed the first pneumatic-tube system in the retail stores of the United States.

January. The Illinois Factory Act, providing for factory inspection, and prohibiting the employment of children under the age of fourteen at night, or for longer than eight hours during the day, was passed as a result of an investigation of child labor conditions in the sweat shops of Chicago.

May 1. The Chicago World's Fair (the World's Columbian Exposition) opened. It was notable for its many modern devices, and its architectural design.

May 5. The panic of 1893 struck the city. Hard times and new violence resulted in Chicago.

September 1. The Armour College of Engineering was opened as a result of a gift by Philip D. Armour.

October 26. Mayor Carter H. Harrison was assassinated one the last day of the World's Fair.

December 4. John Patrick Hopkins was elected mayor in a special election to replace Carter Harrison.

1894 William T. Stead's book, If Christ Came to Chicago, was published. It described the close connection between city politicians, police, and criminals in Chicago.

Graham Taylor founded the Chicago Commons, a very important settlement house in the city.

Nine out of every ten policemen, four-fifths of the fire department, and two-thirds of the school teachers in Chicago were Catholics.

The Chicago Civic Federation conducted a campaign to promote cleaner streets and to organize vacation summer schools. They also campaigned in favor of an extension of civil service laws, against gambling, and the sale of pornography.

January 16. The Field Museum was opened.

February 21. The Chicago Stock Exchange Building was constructed.

March. Chicago had eighty-six miles of cable car tracks, used by four hundred and fifty cars, and operated by eleven power plants.

June 12. The American Railway Union held its first national convention in the city.

June 21-July 20. The Pullman Strike, called by the American Railway Union under Eugene V. Debs took place. When violence broke out, President Grover Cleveland, over the protests of Illinois Governor John P. Altgeld, sent Federal troops into Chicago to restore order. This, combined with a Federal injunction, broke the strike.

November. The Chicago Civic Federation convened a congress on industrial conciliation.

1895

By 1895, Chicago publishers were producing, in volume, more than the publishing houses in any other American city.

The Caxton Club was founded for the purpose of literary study, and for the promotion of the arts pertaining to the production of books.

Julius Rosenwald began the Sears, Roebuck mail order department, which changed the entire method of farm purchasing.

Hull House opened a model playground for children.

The cafeteria line in restaurants was begun in Chicago.

A group known as the Little Room provided a center at Chicago, helping to promote an uplift movement in literature.

January 1. The city government began a civil service system.

April. Carter Harrison II was elected mayor.

November 8. A great automobile race from Evanston to Jackson Park took place. It was sponsored by the Times-Herald.

1896

John Dewey opened the private Laboratory School in the city to test his theories, and teaching methods.

The Municipal Voters' League, organized to bring about political reform in Chicago, began its operations.

April. The Municipal Voters' League accused twenty-six of the thirty-four Aldermen in the city whose terms expired in 1896 as thieves, and helped to prevent the nomination of sixteen candidates whom it did not support.

July 7. The Democratic National Convention was held in the city.

1897

Chicagoans switched to electricity for many purposes in the late 1890's. The Fisk Street Plant, built in 1897 was the first electric power plant in the city.

The Northwestern Elevated Railroad, north from Wilson Street was constructed.

The Chicago Public Library, built at a cost of two million dollars was opened on the lake front.

As the various rapid transit companies built their elevated lines, the famous Loop system was developed in Chicago.

April. Carter Harrison II was re-elected mayor.

1898

A law was passed in Chicago providing for the merit system in the appointment of all city office holders.

De Paul University was opened in the city as a Catholic, co-educational institution.

Chicago settlement house workers in collaboration with Mayor Harrison defeated proposed bills that would have allowed Charles Yerkes to extend streetcar franchises for fifty years.

The first building code adopted in the city went into effect.

January. The City Council merged the Bureau of Street and Alley Cleaning with the Department of Streets in an economy drive.

1899

The Merchants Club succeeded in reforming the city's bookkeeping procedures. The first pawnbroker's society in Chicago was also begun.

The Chicago Juvenile Court, the first of its kind in the United States, was established. Jane Addams and Julia Lathrop had been instrumental in its development.

January. Construction of two and three decker buildings in almost solid rows was begun in the city.

March. The Carson, Pirie, and Scott Building, designed by Louis H. Sullivan, was erected. It was a precursor of the functional form of design.

April. Carter Harrison II was elected mayor for a third term.

July 1. Chicago extended full municipal control over the former town of Pullman.

THE BUSTLING METROPOLIS, 1900-1939

1900

By 1900, the population of the city was 1,698,575.

The average Chicago slums had a density of two hundred and seventy persons per acre, second in congestion only to New York City.

The first "little theater" in the United States was constructed for the Hull House Players.

In 1900, Chicago had twelve daily newspapers. Ten years later the number was eight.

The first phase of the Chicago Sanitary and Ship Canal was completed.

William Randolph Hearst began publishing the Chicago Evening American. About a year later, he opened another newspaper in the city, the Examiner.

The City Homes Association, for the improvement of housing in the city, was begun by Jane Addams and Mrs. Emmons Blaine.

February. Ada and Minna Everleigh opened an establishment called the Everleigh Club, which became the most elegant and costly brothel throughout the entire Middle-West.

1901   April. Carter Harrison II was elected mayor for a fourth straight term.

September 8. Two days after the assassination of President William McKinley, Chicago police arrested hundreds of suspected radicals in the city, including Abraham Isaaks, eidtor of the leading anarchist publication in the city, Free Society.

1902   The City Council adopted a revised building code, which, unfortunately, proved ineffective.

April. An Amendment to the City Charter, extending the mayor's term to four years instead of two, was adopted by the voters.

April 28. An improved tenement house ordinance was passed by the City Council.

1903   The Chicago Women's Trade Union League was organized by Mary McDowell.

A movie studio, Essanay Studio, was opened in the city, but later moved to the West Coast. Several stars, including Francis X. Bushman, Ben Turpin, and Wallace Beery, made pictures in the Chicago studio.

The City Club was established.

April 7. Edward F. Dunne, a Democrat, was elected mayor.

December 31. Chicago witnessed another major diaster, when the Iroquois Theater caught fire. In less than half an hour, five hundred and seventy-one persons, mostly women and children died.

1904   Jane Addams and Harriet Van Der Vaart obtained the cooperation of the Catholic Arch-Bishop and Superintendent of schools in Chicago in enforcing the new compulsory school attendance law.

April. Chicago voters overwhelmingly approved a referendum in favor of municipal ownership of all public utilities. Raymond Robbins led the movement for municipal ownership.

July 12. Chicago's unskilled workers in the stockyards and packing plants went out on strike for higher wages. The strike was not settled until September, when negotiations were conducted between J. Ogden Armour, representing the owners, and Michael Donnelly, and a committee from the labor unions.

1905   Orchestra Hall was opened.

The South Park Commission opened new parks in the city, each with a field house, gymnasium, club rooms, and auditoriums.

The first luncheon club in the United States, the Rotarians, began in the city.

Robert R. McCormick was placed in charge of the Sanitary and Ship Canal Commission.

The Chicago Defender, one of the country's largest Negro newspapers, was founded.

A proposal for a new City Charter was sent to the State Legislature, where it passed both houses, but was defeated by the Chicago voters two years later.

June. The Industrial Workers of the World (I.W.W.) was begun in Chicago at a convention comprised of the Western Federation of Miners, and the American Labor Union.

1906   A convention of representatives of the ethnic groups of Chicago was called by German leaders, where, they agreed to organize as the United Societies for Local Self Government. This organization became an important political force in the city.

Upton Sinclair's novel, The Jungle, was published. It condemned the treatment of Chicago's stockyard workers. It also criticized the evils of the city.

The last cable cars were removed from the streets of Chicago.

Mayor Dunne carried out the state law that required the closing, at one a.m., of all places in the city that sold liquor. The reaction to this attempted order was a series of protest marches and rallies, causing the City Council to amend the state order by issuing certain establishments late permits.

March. The old-fashioned system of administering justice through the justices of the peace was abolished, and a coordinated municipal court was established.

July 17. Gary, Indiana, an outgrowth of Chicago, was incorporated. Outside of Chicago, itself, Gary is the largest city in the Standard Metropolitan Region of Chicago today.

1907

The University of Chicago began the School of Civics and Philanthropy. Graham Taylor and Julia Lathrop were instrumental in its organization.

Charles B. Ball was appointed the head of the Chicago Building Bureau, and for the first time in the city's history, the building codes were enforced.

The present Marshall Field's Department Store Building was constructed.

April 12. Fred A. Busse, a Republican, was elected mayor.

Chicagoans defeated the charter reform referendum.

1908

Frank Lloyd Wright's suburban house, the Robie House, was constructed in a Chicago suburb.

Washington Park Race Track, originally opened in the city during the 1870's, moved to the suburbs.

Mayor Busse settled the battle over Chicago's trolley cars. The city would not take over operation of the companies, but would take fifty-five percent of their earnings. Moreover, a five cent fare was set.

November. Daniel Burnham and his associates submitted the first comprehensive plan for the development and improvement of the city to the Commercial Club. The city government did not act on the plan until the following year.

1909   Gypsy Smith, the revivalist, began an anti-vice crusade, and prompted the first of a series of vice commissions.

A group of Chicago intellectuals, among them Hamlin Garland, Henry Fuller, Lorado Taft, Ralph Clarkson, and Charles F. Browne, organized a club called the Cliff Dwellers, which met on the top floor of Orchestra Hall.

The Carl Schurz High School was erected.

The Chicago Plan Commission was organized. Charles H. Wacker was chosen Chairman, and Daniel Burnham was appointed Chief Architect.

The Blackstone Hotel on East Balboa Avenue was completed.

September. The most serious racial incident in Chicago during the first decade of the Twentieth Century occurred in the Hyde Park section of the city.

1910   The population of Chicago reached 2,185,284, while that of its metropolitan area stood at 3,047,324. Negroes comprised two percent of the total population.

By 1910, one-fifth of all the motion pictures in the world were being made in Chicago.

More than three million cattle and six million hogs entered the Chicago stockyards in this year.

The transit systems in Chicago, carried over 750,000 people a day into the "loop" area.

By 1910, Chicago had established a Lumberman's Exchange, a Livestock Exchange, a Corn Exchange, a Stock Exchange, and several other similar organizations.

Chicago was the leading steel fabricator by this year.

January 10. The Chicago Opera Association was founded, with Andreas Dippel as the Director.

May. The Chicago Vice-Commission was established through the instigation of Gypsy Smith, and Louise De Koven Bowen.

November. As a result of a City Council act, trolley lines outside the city limits were separated from the city's trolley car system.

November 3. The Chicago Opera Company gave its first performance at the Auditorium.

1911

The Chicago Court of Domestic Relations was established.

The Standard Oil Building was erected.

Of the total number of settlement houses in the United States, thirty-four percent were located in Chicago.

January 26. The present day City Hall and County Building was completed after five years of construction.

March. Robert R. McCormick was appointed President of the Chicago Tribune.

April 14. Carter Harrison II was elected mayor for a fifth time on the Progressive Democratic ticket.

August 13-20. The International Aviation Meet was held in the city.

1912

The Chinese began moving into the city. By 1960, the Chinese community reached fifteen hundred people.

Legal prostitution in Chicago was abolished, although vice in the city continued and was now centered in the so-called Black Belt.

Mayor Harrison closed all the bordellos on Michigan Avenue, and even closed the famous Everleigh Club.

The magazine Poetry was begun in Chicago by Harriet Monroe to serve as an organ for new trends in the field.

By 1912, there were two hundred and twenty-seven building and loan associations in the city, with a capital of $19,327,848.

January. The budget of the city was larger than the budget of the State of Illinois as a whole.

March. The Chicago Bailiff's Benevolet Association was founded.

June. The City Council passed an ordinance directed against the smoke nuisance in the air, but attempts to enforce the new restrictions proved ineffective.

1913. January 1. The City Council placed the entire street railway system, almost one thousand miles of track, under one authority, the Chicago Surface Lines.

March. The City Club held a competition for the best model suburb. Walter Burley Griffin, an architect and landscape designer, won first prize.

1914 By 1914, there were sixty-two miles of tunnels under the downtown streets built and operated by the Chicago Tunnel Corporation.

Midway Gardens, one of Chicago's best recreational areas, was built on a design by Frank Lloyd Wright.

Beginning in 1914, tens of thousands of blacks from the South began arriving in Chicago. Their numbers increased steadily during the next five years.

Chicago stood only behind Warsaw and Lodz as one of the largest Polish cities in the world.

April. Chicagoans approved a bond issue to widen Michigan Avenue and to build a new bridge across the river in this area of the city.

August 28. When World War I broke out in Europe, Chicago became the center of neutrality sentiment of the entire country.

September. The Chicago Federation of Labor issued a resolution stating that the "common people" of the city did not want war.

1915	The Association of Commerce and Industry published a smoke abatement study, recommending, among other things, the electrification of all railroad lines entering the city.

The first important attempt to explain the workings of urban life was developed by the "Chicago School" of urban sociology headed by Albion W. Small, William I. Thomas, Charles R. Henderson, and Charles Zueblin at the University of Chicago.

By 1915, the black population of Chicago numbered well over fifty thousand and the black ghetto on the South and West sides of the city had emerged.

April 16. William Hale (Big Bill) Thompson was elected mayor. He was one of the most colorful and corrupt chief executives the city had ever had in its history.

July 24. Chicago experienced another major catastrophe, when the excursion steamer Eastland overturned in the Chicago River, taking 835 people to their deaths.

October. Mayor Thompson issued an order directing that the state Sunday saloon closing laws be enforced. This executive message created an explosion of anger all over the city.

November 7. The United Societies led a protest march and demonstration against the Sunday closing order. Because of all the agitation, by 1916, the order was not enforced. |
| 1916 | In an attempt to please the Germans of the city, Mayor Thompson refused to extend an invitation to Marshal Joffre and a French delegation to the United States to visit the City of Chicago.

The Municipal Pier (later Navy Pier) was constructed to handle the increased lake-passenger and packet-freight vessels. It was a huge structure, reaching three thousand feet into the water.

As a result of World War I, anti-Germanism grew in Chicago, even to the extent that the Bismarck Hotel changed its name to the Hotel Randolph, and Kaiserhof became the Atlantic Hotel. |

May 11. The Wiebolt Department Store was opened.

1917

The Boston Store, seventeen stories high, was completed.

The original two star flag of the City of Chicago was designed by Wallace Rice, and adopted by the municipality.

January 26. The band of New Orleans, the first jazz band in Chicago, opened an engagement at Riesenweber's Cabaret.

April 6. Chicagoans exhibited great patriotism when the United States declared war on Germany. All talk of neutrality disappeared. The years of World War I in Chicago were tense, however, as a result of the city's large German-American population.

September. The Chicago License Committee approved a measure allowing a special committee, composed of the Chief of Police, the Corporation Counsel, and the Chairman of the License Committee, to issue saloon licenses.

1918

November 11. The Art Club of Chicago was established.

Although American participation in World War I was quite popular in the city, the Armistice brought crowds of people into the downtown streets.

1919

More than twenty thousand street cars, and over one hundred and thirty thousand other types of vehicles entered the Loop on each working day in 1919.

The Field Museum of Natural History was constructed.

Chicago builders benefitted from a decision rendered by Judge Kennesaw Mountain Landis, which allowed employers to reduce the hourly wages of their employees by twelve and a half percent, ended all sympathy strikes, revised the laws concerning materials for construction, and decreed compulsory arbitration on all matters involving labor unions.

Mary Garden became the impressario of the Chicago Opera, the first woman in the United States to achieve such a position.

The terms of the Aldermen of Chicago were increased from one to two years.

April. William H. Thompson was re-elected mayor.

June. The City Council passed the Lake Front Ordinance, which provided for larger lake shore improvement.

July 27-31. A bloody race riot took place in the city, caused when a black youth swam onto the "white beach" along the lake front. The riot raged for four days, and left fifteen whites and twenty-three blacks dead, 178 whites and 342 blacks injured, as well as millions of dollars worth of property damaged.

October 28. The National Prohibition Enforcement Act was passed. It went into effect on January 16, 1920. Chicagoans, strenuously opposed the law.

1920   Chicago's population stood at 2,701,705 while its metropolitan area was 3,858,818.

In 1920, Chicago was the home of well over 1,000,000 Catholics, 800,000 foreign-born immigrants, 125,000 Jews, 200,000 first and second generation Bohemians, and 110,000 blacks.

The Drake Hotel was erected.

The new Michigan Avenue Bridge was finally completed.

By 1920, Chicago contained one hundred freight yards.

Mayor Thompson's bill to levy a five cent fare on all of Chicago's surface lines was defeated in the State Legislature. At the same time, a new tax package was also turned down.

February. Mayor Thompson, without the approval of the City Council, set up the office of Law Enforcement Commissioner, whose function it was to administer all the Federal and State prohibition laws. John Henry Williamson was appointed commissioner.

April. An Amendment to the State Constitution, which would have permanently limited the representation of the city in the state legislature, in exchange for home rule, was defeated by Chicago voters.

May. A public celebration was held when the widening of Michigan Avenue, and the opening of the new double-leaf bascule bridge across the river at North Michigan Avenue were completed.

"Big Jim" Colosimo, head of bootlegging and vice in Chicago was murdered, and the crime syndicate in the city was taken over by Johnny Torio.

June 8. The Republican National Convention met in Chicago, and nominated Warren G. Harding for the presidency. Actually Harding was chosen by the Republican bosses at a private conference in a smoke-filled room at the Blackstone Hotel.

1921

The City Council reorganized the Chicago Police Department by reducing the control of the mayor and the chief of police over the precincts, and by increasing the autonomy of the individual police captains.

February. The City Council passed a resolution requesting state and federal officials to take steps to bring about a wine and beer amendment, so as to temper, somewhat, the Volstead Act.

June 1. The first branch of the Ku Klux Klan in Chicago was established by C.W. Love, Grand Goblin of the Domain of the Great Lakes. His headquarters were located on Clark Street.

September. Former Mayor Dunne, and attorney, Clarence Darrow, headed a National Unity Council to seek legislation to crush the Klan.

September 19. The City Council adopted a resolution to rid Chicago of the Ku Klux Klan.

1922

The Straus (Continental Companies) Building on Michigan Avenue was opened.

The Chicago City Council sent a letter to all cities in the nation with a population of 25,000 or more, to demand a new national amendment that would legalize the sale of wine and beer.

May 21. The City Council voted to oppose any expenditures of city funds to enforce the prohibition law.

June 21. The American Unity League, whose purpose was to rid Chicago of the Ku Klux Klan, was founded by Robert H. Shepherd, Grady K. Rutledge, and Joseph G. Keller.

August. The seven story, Popular Mechanics Building was completed.

A huge rally was held in the city to protest the prohibition amendment. Many important anti-prohibition leaders, including Alfred E. Smith of New York, attended.

August 25. New traffic signals were installed on most of the city's more congested streets and intersections.

1923

The London Guarantee Building (now the Stone Container) was erected.

April 5. A new zoning ordinance was adopted by the City Council, which limited building at the street line to a height of 265 feet, though setback towers could be added above this height. The ordinance also reserved large areas along the main streets for commercial use.

June. As early as 1923, Rufus C. Dawes proposed the holding of another World's Fair in Chicago to celebrate the city's centennial. Ten years later, Dawes became the president of the Chicago Century of Progress Fair.

November 6. William Dever defeated William Thompson for the mayoralty, as the reform of city government was desired.

1924

Union Station was opened for public use. It was built with public and private funds.

The Tribune Tower, a landmark of Chicago, was erected. Raymond Hood was the designer.

Richard Loeb and Nathan Leopold murdered fourteen year old Robert Franks. The defense of the murderers by Clarence Darrow allowed them to escape execution. They were both sentenced to life imprisonment.

Al Capone, head of the Chicago underworld, moved out of Chicago, and established his headquarters in a suburb, Cicero, Illinois.

By 1924, despite the prohibition law, there were fifteen breweries in operation in Chicago, and 20,000 retail outlets for the illegal sale of beer and alcoholic beverages.

The Wrigley Building was erected.

More than 30,000 employees worked in Chicago's printing and publishing establishments, which had a total value of $270,000,000.

The Chicago Rapid Transit Company united all the elevated lines in the city.

February. The disintegration of the Ku Klux Klan in Chicago, was almost complete by this time.

November 10. A serious gang war broke out in Chicago, when Dion O'Banion, a rival of Al Capone, was assassinated by Capone's allies, the Genna brothers. Within four months, four of the seven Genna brothers were murdered by O'Banion's allies.

1925

South Water Street Market, the city's principal center for wholesale produce, was relocated to make way for the new super highway, Wacker Drive.

The Chicago Zoning Commission reported that more than twice as many Chicagoans lived in apartments as in conventional homes.

1926

In 1926, the city contained 341,000 automobiles and 18,000 motor vehicles of other kinds.

Samuel Insull asked the City Council to allow him to build and operate a subway. The Council turned him down.

In 1926, the city's department stores showed total sales of $361,000,000 or 18.2 percent of Chicago's combined retail business.

Soldier Field, a $6,000,000 structure, was opened as an all purpose outdoor stadium.

April. By April, 1926, there were twenty-nine gang killings in Chicago. Not a single conviction for murder was obtained.

July 21. The Illinois-Central Railroad began the electic operations of its trains into the city.

1927 The Buckingham Fountain was installed in Grant Park. It was a gift to the city from Kate Buckingham, in memory of her brother Clarence, who had been a director of the Art Institute.

A project to straighten a bend of the Chicago River in the center of the city was completed.

The city government began a campaign to force houseboaters living on the Chicago River to find new locations for their craft. This was part of the movement to beautify the city, and especially the river.

Construction began on the Lief Ericson Drive along the lake front.

Property reassessment for the purpose of increased tax revenues was undertaken in the city. It was not completed until 1930, and as a result, many property owners in Chicago did not pay taxes for three years.

The first municipal airport (later called Midway Airport) was dedicated and opened for use.

April. William H. Thompson was again elected mayor. This was his third term.

May. As soon as Thompson returned to office, Al Capone moved back to Chicago from Cicero. To a very large extent, Capone paid for "Big Bill's" campaign.

1928 Mayor Thompson threatened to punch King George of England in the "snoot" if he came to Chicago. This statement was a political maneuver to please the Irish and German voters of the city.

The Julius Rosenwald Fund contributed money to construct the Michigan Boulevard Apartments, consisting of 421 units. It was intended for the Negro South Side.

January. The City Council enacted an ordinance banning parking on the downtown streets in a move to alleviate the traffic and congestion in the city's business district.

1929   The world famous Merchandise Mart was opened. At the time, it was the world's largest building.

The volume of traffic on the Chicago Surface Lines reached its height, when 890,000,000 fares were paid during this year.

The Medinah Athletic Club, now the Sheraton-Chicago Hotel was constructed.

The Shedd Aquarium was opened to the public.

Emory Thomason began publishing the Chicago Illustrated Times.

February 14. The St. Valentine's Day Massacre took place, during which seven of Al Capone's enemies were machine gunned to death in a Chicago garage.

October. The panic of 1929 struck the city, bringing on hard times in Chicago for the next eight years.

November. As the panic worsened, Chicago banks announced that they would accept no more warrants.

November 4. The Civic Opera began its performances in a a new building on North Wacker Drive. This project was initiated and financed by Samuel Insull.

1930   The population of Chicago was well over 3,000,000 people, while its metropolitan area numbered close to 4,700,000.

In 1930, Polish residents of the city represented 13.7 percent of the total population, while Bohemians accounted for 17.8 percent.

By 1930, Chicago had a dozen foreign language dailies, with a circulation of well over 21,000.

The present Board of Trade Building was completed.

Regular airline passenger service was established between Chicago and Salt Lake City, and Chicago and San Francisco.

The corner of State and Madison Streets in Chicago's Loop was leased at a rate of $50,000 a foot, a rate equal to $21,789,000 an acre.

May. The Adler Planetarium was opened in Grant Park. It completed an impressive cultural center, and was the first planetarium built in the country. In addition to the planetarium, the park's 200 acres also contained the Field Museum and the Shedd Aquarium.

June 9. Jake Lingle, a police reporter for the Chicago Tribune, was murdered.

July 14. Jake Zuta, a well-known gangster, was shot to death while in the custody of police, by fellow-gangsters.

September. Large numbers of unemployed men and women came to Chicago as the depression deepened. A shanty town appeared at the foot of Randolph Street, derisively called Hooverville.

October. As the City of Chicago was in desperate straits as a result of the depression, Governor Louis L. Emmerson of Illinois, established a Commission on Unemployment and Relief, whose main function was to raise $5,000,000 from private sources for relief in Chicago. The drive was not very successful.

November. Chicagoans approved a $5,000,000 bond issue to be used for road building and street improvements.

1931

Al Capone was found guilty of income tax evasion, and sentenced to prison for ten years.

As the depression grew worse, the Oak Forest Poorhouse was forced to turn away 19,000 transients in the city.

The Chicago Bailiff's Office evicted nearly 1,400 depression-poor families from their homes.

Through most of 1931, and part of 1932, Chicago's public school teachers were not paid as a result of a shortage of funds in the city treasury due to the depression.

April. Anton J. Cermak, a Democrat was elected mayor. He was the first Czech elected to such an office in the United States.

May 1. There was $670,000,000 in unpaid taxes in the city as a result of the depression.

CHRONOLOGY

June 3. The City of Chicago owed $4,500,000 in unpaid bills, and the Board of Education a like amount.

August. A series of "eviction riots" took place, during which several persons were killed, and many others wounded.

October 15. By the middle of the month, 624,000 persons were unemployed in the city. This situation got worse.

1932

Mayor Cermak began negotiations with the Reconstruction Finance Corporation (R.F.C.) for a loan in order to build the Chicago subway.

June 27-30. The Democratic National Convention met in Chicago.

August. In an economy drive, 1,085 city jobs were eliminated at an annual saving of $2,483,000. By November, another 1,492 city employees were discharged.

September. Of Chicago's 228 banks, only 51 were still open.

October. By October, statistics showed that Chicago was one of the hardest hit of the major American cities during the depression. More than 750,000 Chicagoans were unemployed, and the weekly cost of relief was $1,500,000. In addition, rents dropped drastically, and wages fell.

November. The City of Chicago received a series of loans from the Reconstruction Finance Corporation for public works improvements.

November 8. In the presidential election, Chicagoans voted overwhelmingly for Franklin D. Roosevelt.

December. Frank Nitti, "The Enforcer" of the Capone mob, was shot in a police raid. He was hit three times, but did not die.

1933

The loan-grant from the Public Works administration (P.W.A.) helped Chicago build a new sewage system.

The Sanitary and Ship Canal, linking the Great Lakes System, the Mississippi River System, and Chicago was officially opened by Mayor Cermak.

In order to raise additional revenue, the State Legislature enated a sales tax for Chicago.

February 15. Mayor Cermake was shot in Miami by an assassin, Guisseppe Zangara, who was trying to kill President Roosevelt while he was making a speech in the Florida city.

March 6. Anton Cermak died in Miami. His body was brought to Chicago, and the most spectacular funeral demonstration in the city's history took place. Edward J. Kelly was named acting mayor to finish Cermak's unexpired term.

May 27. The second Chicago World's Fair opened. It was designed by Joseph Urban, and was called "A Century of Progress."

The Crusade of Mercy (originally the Community Fund) was established.

The Field Building was constructed.

April. Under an act approved by popular referendum, the Chicago Park District was established. It was a separate commission not subject to City Council control.

Chicago alderman's terms were increased from two to four years. Within a few years time, their terms were reduced, once again, to two years.

December 5. Chicago voters went overwhelmingly for the amendment to repeal prohibition.

1935   Rents in Chicago were only one-half of what they had been in the 1923-25 period.

April 1. Edward J. Kelly was elected mayor in his own right.

1937   May 30. A group of union demonstrators, marching in front of the gates of Republic Steel in South Chicago, were fired upon by police, resulting in the death of four of the men, and the wounding of eight-four others.

September. The United States Housing Authority began a

series of slum clearance and housing projects in Chicago.

October 5. President Roosevelt dedicated the Outer Drive Bridge, which connected the main stream of Chicago city traffic with the super highway along Lake Michigan.

1938   May. The Jane Addams Housing Project, totalling 304 new units was opened. The Federal government allotted $65,950,000 for this housing development.

1939   The Chicago Land Use Survey found 76,000 housing units in the city in need of major repairs, or unfit for use.

The old Chicago Plan Commission was reorganized. It was to play a much larger role in the operations and development of city government.

April. Edward J. Kelly was re-elected mayor.

CHICAGO: WORLD METROPOLIS, 1940-1970

1940   The population of Chicago stood at 3,200,000 while the Chicago Metropolitan Area reached 4,800,000.

By 1940, the Black population of Chicago increased by more than 43,000 people, an increase of 18.7 percent as compared to 1930.

The Illinois Institute of Technology, located in Chicago, was opened.

1941   The Frances Cabrini Homes were erected. The project cost $3,700,000, including the demolition of the blighted areas.

The Chicago Sun was established by Marshall Field.

January 18. The Ida Wells Housing Project, to provide dwellings for 1,662 low income black families, was opened. This development covered nearly forty-seven acres.

December 7. The entry of the United States into World War II, caused Chicagoans to unite behind the nation's war effort. Chicago's citizens took great pride in their support of the government. Many of the city's buildings and resources were turned over to the war effort.

December 21. A tent city was constructed for soldiers undergoing training at Fort Sheridan.

1942 Robert Maynard Hutchins, the President of the University of Chicago, was primarily responsible for bringing the government's atomic energy project to the city.

December 2. Enrico Fermi directed the first atomic chain reaction at the University of Chicago, where the first nuclear reactor in the United States had been constructed.

1943 The Chicago Plan Commission called for the total demolition of twenty-three square miles of blighted and near blighted residential areas, and the start of massive urban renewal projects in these sections of the city.

The Chicago Housing Authority opened the 834 unit Robert H. Brooks Homes on the Near North Side.

A new State Street Subway was finally completed. This was the first underground subway in Chicago, and a part of the master plan to construct a system of subways and superhighways radiating away from downtown.

April. Edward Kelly was re-elected mayor for a third term.

1945 By 1945, Chicago was the second largest black city in the world, only New York's Harlem exceeding it in size. There were more than 300,000 blacks within Chicago's "blackbelt."

Beginning in 1945, many new enterprises located their factories and offices outside of Chicago, while a number of established Chicago operations moved into suburban settings.

One-quarter of the national employment in the production of radio and television sets was found in metropolitan Chicago.

By 1945, Midway Airport was handling 80,000 planes and 1,300,000 passengers annually.

1946 The Argonne National Laboratory, located twenty miles southwest of the Loop was established by the Federal government as a center for atomic research.

The Chicago Community Inventory was created by a grant from the Wiebolt Foundation. Philip M. Hauser became its director. This organization was primarily interested in human ecology.

1947   The Chicago Land Commission was created as a result of the Illinois Blighted Areas Act, for the purposes of slum clearance and urban renewal.

April. Martin Kennelly was elected mayor.

1948   December. A huge Railroad Exposition and Fair was held in the city during the winter of 1948-49.

1949   The old Chicago Juvenile Court was transformed into a new Family Court, which became a branch of the Circuit Court.

The Midwest Stock Exchange was established in the city, as a result of a merger between the old Chicago Stock Exchange, and the exchanges located in Cleveland, St. Louis, and Minneapolis-St. Paul.

The Mid-West Inter-Library Center was established in Chicago to provide participating midwestern universities with research materials.

The Greyhound Bus Terminal Building on Randolph Street was opened, and Chicago became the national headquarters for this important company.

1950   The population of Chicago rached 3,621,000 while its metropolitan area grew to 5,600,000.

In the decade between 1940 and 1950, Chicago annexed 41.1 square miles of land to its metropolitan area.

The city hit a peak of employment in 1950, when 593,086 persons had jobs in the manufacturing establishments of the city. Ten years later, employment dropped by 90,000.

Dearborn Homes was the first high-rise public housing project completed after World War II.

The Department of Housing announced that twenty-eight percent of all dwellings in the city were to be included within the dilapidated category.

1951 The New York Life Insurance Company invested in a large middle-income, racially integrated housing project; the Lake Meadows Development. The first buildings in the complex were completed in 1953.

The Milwaukee Avenue, Lake Street, Dearborn Street Subway was opened for public use.

By 1951, one out of every four doctors in the United States had taken part of his training at one of the hospitals within the West Side Medical Center Complex in Chicago.

April. Martin Kennelly was re-elected mayor.

1952 July 7-11. The Republican National Convention was held in the city.

1953 Chicago surpassed Pittsburgh in the value of its manufacture of primary metals.

The city government published a new planning manual, Chicago Tomorrow. It included plans for a number of Chicago's future developments.

Martin P. Durkin, vice-president of the Chicago Building Trades Council, was appointed Secretary of Labor by President Dwight D. Eisenhower.

March. Fritz Reiner was appointed conductor of the Chicago Symphony Orchestra.

July. Richard J. Daley was elected Chairman of the Cook County Democratic Central Committee, the most powerful political organization in the Chicago metropolitan area.

September. The City of Chicago created a Municipal Parking Authority.

1954 Cudahy meat packing company moved its four plants out of the city.

The Lyric Opera Company was organized in Chicago.

By 1954, the Chicago metropolitan area was producing one-quarter of the nation's total output of iron and steel.

Chicago became the first center of a new transportation innovation, "piggyback" traffic (trailer trains).

The University of Illinois decided to locate its Chicago branch at what is now called the Chicago Circle Campus. It was located at a series of main intersections in the heart of one of the poorer sections of the city.

1955   Chicago's Department of Urban Renewal was created.

The Prudential Building, the first new office building in Chicago since 1934, was completed. The construction of this building set off a wave of new office-building construction in the city. Among the new edifices that were subsequently erected were the U.S. Gypsum Building, the Brunswick Building, the Hartford Insurance Building, and the Continental Center.

The Northeastern Metropolitan Local Services Commission (Randolph Commission) was established to provide services needed for cooperative activity in the Chicago metropolitan area.

April 5. Richard J. Daley was elected mayor, He was the "boss" of the most powerful Democratic political machine in the country.

August. Chicago's sales tax was raised, and a new utility tax also went into operation.

November 2. The enlargement of the Calumet-Sag Channel was begun to facilitate the movement of ocean-going vessels into the Port of Chicago.

1956   Mayor Daley hired more policemen and firemen for the city, doubled construction shifts on the east-west expressway, and began new street lighting and paving projects in the city.

Midway Airport was unable to handle the volume of air traffic coming into the city. As a result, O'Hare International Airport was opened. It soon became the busiest airport in the world.

The Eisenhower Expressway was constructed.

August 13-17. The Democratic National Nominating Convention was held in Chicago.

November 3. Chicagoans passed a huge bond issue to raise funds for the start of a series of public works projects. The biggest expenditures were to go to O'Hare International Airport, the construction of new bridges and street crossings, streetlights, sewers, and lake docking facilities.

1957

Edwin Berry, the new executive director of the Chicago Urban League, charged that Chicago was the most residentially segregated city in the United States. And, by 1957, Chicago had the largest black ghetto of any city in the United States.

A merger of the City of Chicago, and the Chicago Park District occurred for the purposes of greater efficiency, maintenance and security.

Life Magazine charged that Chicago police were the most corrupt in the nation.

January 1. Chicago reconstituted its planning agency as a full fledged executive department, and retained the old planning commission only as an advisory board.

July 1. Beginning in 1957, sole responsibility for the preparation of the city's budget was given to the mayor.

1958

The Jewish Federation of Metropolitan Chicago was founded.

The number of wards in Chicago was increased from thirty-five to fifty, but representation from each ward was reduced from two to one alderman.

The 1,900 unit Cabrini Extension Project of the Chicago Housing Authority was completed.

November. Chicago aldermen's terms were once again increased from two to four years.

1959

Ben Adamowski, the States' Attorney, uncovered two major scandals in Chicago. The first concerned the "fixing" of parking tickets, while the second scandal showed that bail bondsmen were getting their money back from the courts after their customers jumped bail.

The Armour meat packing plant in Chicago was closed.

April. Richard Daley was re-elected mayor.

April 16. The <u>Johan Willem Friso,</u> of the Oranje Line, docked at Chicago. It was the first ship to arrive at Chicago directly from overseas.

June. Queen Elizabeth of Great Britain visited Chicago as a guest of City Hall.

June 26. The St. Lawrence Seaway opened. Chicago's marine commerce benefitted from this event.

August. The Pan-American Games (an international track meet) was held in Chicago.

September. The Chicago White Sox professional baseball team won the American League pennant, but lost to the Los Angeles Dodgers in the World Series.

1960

The population of Chicago declined somewhat to stand at 3,550,404, but, at the same time, Chicago's metropolitan area grew to 6,794,461, indicating a definite movement out of the central city to the suburbs.

As late as 1960, one out of every five white Chicagoans was foreign-born. The Poles comprised the largest single ethnic group in the city, while the Japanese, with 11,375 people, were the largest oriental group. Seventy-three percent of Chicago's foreign-born (600,000) still lived in the central city rather than the suburbs.

By 1960, the Chicago Standard Metropolitan Area comprised a total of 1,060 local governments.

A great police scandal rocked Chicago, as it was disclosed by State's Attorney Adamowski that members of the Chicago police department were working with a gang of Chicago burglars.

February. In a major reshuffling of the Chicago police department, Orlando Wilson, chairman of the Criminology Department of the University of California, was appointed by Mayor Daley as Chief of Police of Chicago. Wilson was the first out-of-stater to ever be named to this position.

	May. The first electric power generated by atomic energy entered Chicago's electrical power system.
1961	In 1961, a Federally sponsored development for the elderly, Washington Park Homes, was opened.
	The campus for the Chicago branch of the University of Illinois was begun in that section of the city known as the "Valley," largely inhabited by Italians.
1962	November 6. Chicagoans defeated a $66,000,000 bond issue referendum intended for public works improvements.
1963	By 1963, there was one automobile for every three people in the city.
	April. Richard Daley easily won re-election to the mayoralty.
	September. Blacks of Chicago, led by the Woodlawn Organization, came downtown to picket City Hall for better schools in the black neighborhoods. After the picketing, school boycotts were organized, and tens of thousands of black children were kept at home.
1964	The Sara Lee Bakeries in a Chicago suburb, Deerfield, were opened.
	Bertrand Goldberg's Marina City, consisting of apartments, offices, restaurants, garages, a television studio, marina, and a bank, was completed. Its circular twin towers have become a landmark in Chicago.
	February. A rapid transit system was organized jointly by the village of Skokie and the Chicago Transit Authority with federal financial assistance.
	July 18-August 30. Periodic episodes of severe rioting by ghetto blacks in Chicago took place.
1965	By 1965, only four daily newspapers were being published in Chicago.
	Over half of the industrial jobs in the Chicago metropolitan area were to be found outside the city.

The campus of the University of Illinois at Chicago Circle was officially opened.

As late as 1965, Chicago was still being served by twenty trunk line railroads, which constituted close to one-half of the nation's total railway mileage.

The Chicago Civic Center was completed.

The Ford City Development, Chicago's largest shopping center was opened. Part of the complex was also used for the creation of an industrial district.

As a result of the movement of several of the large meat packing companies out of Chicago, by 1965, the city was no longer the nation's most important meat packing center.

The Federal Building, a modern skyscraper, was erected.

August. Four nights of rioting by Chicago's ghetto blacks took place. About eighty people were injured.

1966   Senator Paul H. Douglas of Illinois succeeded in getting a federal commitment to develop portions of the lake shore for recreation and conservation purposes.

June. The Puerto Rican section of Chicago in the northwest part of the city erupted into a riot.

July. Another black riot broke out on the West Side. Sniperfire, looting and arson occurred, and the Illinois National Guard was called in by Mayor Daley. The mayor placed the blame for the violence on Dr. Martin Luther King Jr., who had come to Chicago to discuss integration with Daley.

October. A "Summit Agreement" was reached by Mayor Daley and Dr. King concerning open housing. However, it was not an official document, had no legal standing, and was not carried out. It did, however, end the crisis of marches and protests in Chicago, by blacks, for the time being.

December. A comprehensive plan for the development of Chicago was prepared by the Department of Development and Planning.

1967   Chicago was named as one of sixty-three cities to take part in the Model Cities Program of the federal government's Department of Housing and Urban Development.

The Museum of Contemporary Art was opened.

In 1967, over 27,000,000 passengers arrived and departed through O'Hare International Airport.

The Hyde Park Urban Renewal Project was completed.

Dilapidated housing in the city dropped to 10 percent of all units in Chicago.

Police Chief Wilson retired, and was replaced by James Conlisk, whose father had been an old friend of Mayor Daley.

January. McCormick Place, Chicago's largest exhibition hall was destroyed by a huge fire. It had been an object of controversy ever since it opened in 1960, especially among conservationists who believed the structure was ruining the lake front.

April. Richard Daley was re-elected mayor for a fourth term, easily defeating his Republican opponent John Warner. In 1971, he was once again elected mayor for an unprecedented fifth term. (Four year terms.)

1968

South Commons, a large, privately developed high rise and town house project on South Michigan Avenue, costing $20,000,000, was completed.

By 1968, more than a third of Chicago's non-white population was listed by the census as middle class.

April 15. Mayor Daley issued a "shoot on sight" order to the police in an attempt to stop the violence, looting and burning of Chicago's West Side by blacks, who were rioting in reaction to the assassination of Martin Luther King in Memphis, Tennessee on April 14, 1968.

April 27. A battle took place at Civic Center Plaza between police and peace groups, who were holding a march and rally. Several people were hurt, others arrested and the police were guilty of extreme brutality.

May. A strike of the International Brotherhood of Electrical Workers against Illinois Bell Telephone Company severely disrupted telephone and broadcasting communications. The strike was not settled until September 21.

July. The City Council extended provisions of its open-housing ordinance to ban discrimination by anyone engaged in the sale or rental of housing.

August 17. Transportation in the city was seriously hampered by a drivers and mechanics strike that idled 80 percent of Chicago's taxicabs. Sporadic disorders finally broke out into severe rioting on August 28.

August 26-30. The Democratic National Convention met in Chicago. Riots and street fighting erupted between thousands of anti-war demonstrators who had come to Chicago to protest the Vietnam situation, and Chicago police. Pitched battles raged in several of the city's parks and throughout the downtown streets. Scores were injured and arrested, while a considerable amount of property damage was done to several sections of the city.

September. A United States District Court ordered that Chicago's wards be redistricted according to the one man, one vote principle, in time for the aldermanic elections in November 1971.

1969 The Weathermen faction of the Students for a Democratic Society (S.D.S.) staged their so-called days of rage in Chicago, that included a window breaking spree in the Loop area.

By 1969, the city's loss of manufacturing enterprises reached almost 200.

Spearheaded by the Coalition for United Community Action (civic and religious groups in the black community), an attack was made on the hiring practices of the building trades unions, and the construction industry. Difficulties persisted throughout the year.

By 1969, Chicago's park system encompassed 6,880 acres of land, divided into 486 parks.

Overseas ship arrivals at the Port of Chicago numbered 137 in 1969.

The value of new construction projects in the city by the end of 1969, reached $565,926,410.

The Mayor's Committee on Economics and Cultural Development began a new program to promote new areas for industrial development, and to attract investment.

The President's Commission on Violence (The Walker Report), headed by a Chicagoan, Daniel Walker, was extremely critical of the Chicago police in their actions at the time of the Democratic National Convention riots. In a scathing denunciation, the Report stated that much of the violence was the result of a "police riot." Mayor Daley criticized the report, and defended the actions of his police department.

Two rapid transit systems were added to the city's transit network, providing high speed transportation to Chicago's Loop area.

In 1969, 927 conventions and trade shows were held in the city. Almost 1,500,000 delegates from out of town attended these meetings, and delegate expenditures were estimated at more than $400,000,000.

By 1969, there were 37,587 dwellings in the city.

April. Construction began on a new McCormick Place on the same site as the old one, which had been destroyed by fire two years earlier. Mayor Daley and a number of Chicago ecologists and conservationists battled over the convention center's reconstruction. The mayor won out, but the issue has remained a serious bone of contention ever since.

May 22-23. Chicago public school teachers staged a two day walkout for the first time in the city's history.

September 15. The City Council agreed to transfer to the school board the city's share of the state income tax for educational purposes. This action prevented another teacher's strike.

September 24. The trial of the so-called Chicago Eight began in the courtroom of Judge Julius Hoffmann. These eight defendants, including Bobby Seale, Rennie Davis, and David Dellinger, were indicted for inciting the August riot at the Democratic National Convention. The trial dragged on for almost a year, and was quite sensational, mainly as a result of the actions of Judge Hoffmann, and the defense attorney, William Kunstler.

December 4. Led by Edward Hanrahan, the State's Attorney, Chicago police staged a pre-dawn raid on Black Panther headquarters in Chicago. Bursting into a Panther apartment, the police shot and killed two Panthers, Fred Hampton, and Mark Clark, while wounding four others, The police claimed that the Panthers were armed, and had fired first, but conflicting evidence led to a widespread call for an independent investigation of police activities.

1970　　The Standard Metropolitan Area of Chicago grew to almost 8,000,000 people, but the population of the City of Chicago itself declined again, dropping to 3,329,000.

George Solti was named musical director, and Carlo Maria Guilini was appointed principal guest conductor of the Chicago Symphony Orchestra.

By 1970, there were 957,212 passenger vehicles in the city, while 70,327 trucks, and 12,128 motorcycles clogged the city's streets.

Work was begun on the construction of the Sears, Roebuck Building, which, when completed, will be the tallest building in the world.

The John Hancock Center Building 100 stories and 1,105 feet high was completed and opened.

By 1970, Chicago's extensive super highway system was essentially completed. The Edens and Kennedy highways were built, north and northwest; the Eisenhower highway, went west; the Stevenson and Dan Ryan expressways went south and southwest; while the Calumet and Kingery were built to the southeast.

More than sixty killings were attributed to Chicago street gangs in 1970.

Four Chicago police officers were murdered by Chicago street gang members.

The church of a black minister, who had been working among gang youths in Chicago, was firebombed and almost completely destroyed.

By 1970, more than 20,000 students were commuting to the Chicago Circle Campus of the University of Illinois.

January 21. A special coroner's jury ruled that the deaths of the Black Panthers, killed in the 1969 police raid, were completely justified.

February 18. The conspiracy trial of the Chicago Seven (originally Chicago Eight) was ended. The jury returned a series of controversial verdicts, which imposed relatively light sentences on the defendents, pleasing neither conservatives or liberals.

March. Mayor Daley was re-elected head of the Cook County Democratic Party, a post he had held continuously since 1953.

June. Chicago was pushed to the brink of a major crisis in health care, with the threatened shutdown of Cook County Hospital, the only source of health care for most of the city's poor inhabitants.

July 8. The Chicago Transit Authority increased its basic fare on all transportation lines to forty-five cents. This was the fourth increase in the fare since 1961.

September. The Chicago Board of Education began to carry out a faculty desegregation plan under the threat of a federal suit, and a counteraction by the Chicago Teachers' Union.

November. The fifty wards from which the Chicago City Council members were elected were redistricted.

December. A special state Grand Jury began an investigation into the Black Panther police raid of 1969.

DOCUMENTS

The principal aim of this documents section is to bring together in convenient and usable form a body of selections that will serve as an effective tool for an initial understanding of the history of the city of Chicago. The material assembled here will help students attain some insights into the almost one hundred and fifty years of Chicago's fascinating history. While the series of documents gathered in this volume does not presume to be the final word on the documentary history of the Windy City, they will help the student to discover the vividness and excitement of the subject.

The author has attempted to present as wide a spectrum of documents as possible. They include descriptions of the city written by contemporaries, newspaper accounts of particularly interesting incidents in Chicago's history, and a number of public documents, such as city charters, proclamations of the mayor, city ordinances, and the like. Obviously much more could have been included within any volume on the development of Chicago, but space limitations precluded the author from selecting additional materials. Space limitations aside, the documents that follow will act as an excellent starting point for the student interested in pursuing further the study of Chicago's growth and development.

Several libraries contain first rate collections of primary materials on the subject. The University of Chicago has one of the best repositories on the history of the city, while the University of Illinois, and Northwestern University both contain much valuable research materials and papers. Last, but certainly not least, is the Municipal Reference Library of the city of Chicago, which houses, probably, the best assemblage of public and private documents on the subject.

THE FIRST CHARTER OF THE TOWN OF CHICAGO - 1831

In 1831, the Illinois General Assembly passed a law for the incorporation of towns in the state. Under this Act, Chicago was first incorporated, although the town was not officially organized until 1833.

(Source: Edmund J. James, The Charters of the City of Chicago, Part I, The Early Charters, 1833-1837. Chicago, 1898.)

Section 1. Be it enacted by the people of the State of Illinois, represented in the General Assembly, That whenever the white males over the age of twenty-one years, being residents of any town in this state, containing not less than 150 inhabitants, shall wish to become incorporated for the better regulation of their internal police, it shall be lawful for the said residents, who may have resided six months therein, or who shall be the owner of any freehold property therein, to assemble themselves together, in public meeting, at the courthouse or other place in said town, and when so assembled, they may proceed to choose a president and clerk of the meeting from among their number, both of whom shall be sworn, or affirmed, by any person authorized to administer oaths, faithfully to discharge the trust reposed in them as president and clerk of said meeting; provided, however, that at least ten days' public notice of the time and place of holding such meeting, shall have been previously given by advertising in some newspaper of the town, or by setting up written notices, in at least three of the most public places in such town.

Sec. 2 The residents, as aforesaid, of any town having assembled as directed in the first section of this act, may proceed to decide by vote, viva voce, whether they will be incorporated or not, and the president and clerk, after their votes are given in, shall certify under their hands, the number of votes, in favor of being incorporated, and the number against being incorporated; and if it shall appear that two-thirds of the votes present are in favor of being incorporated, the president and clerk shall deliver a certificate of the state of the polls to the board of trustees, to be elected as hereinafter provided.

Sec. 3 Whenever the qualified voters, under this act, of any town, shall have decided in the manner herein provided, that they wish to be incorporated, it shall be the duty of the clerk of the meeting, at which they may so decide, to give at least five days' previous public notice to the said voters, to assemble at the courthouse, or some other public place in such town, on a day to be named in such notice, to elect by viva voce vote, five residents and freeholders of such town, for trustees of the same, who shall hold their office for one year, and until other trustees are chosen and qualified; at which first election, the president and clerk of the first meeting shall preside, or in case of the absence of either of them, some suitable person shall be appointed by the electors present to fill such vacancy or vacancies. And at every succeeding election for president and trustees, the preceding board of trustees shall direct the manner in which the same shall be conducted.

Sec. 4 The board of trustees of any town elected agreeably to the provisions of this act, shall choose a president out of their own body, and the president and trustees aforesaid, and their successors in office, shall thenceforth be considered in law and equity, a body corporate and politic, by the name and style of "the president and trustees of the town of --------," and by such name and style shall be forever able and capable in law and equity to sue and be sued, to plead and be impleaded, to answer and be answered unto, defend and be defended in all manner of suits, actions, plaints, pleas, causes, matters, and demands, of whatever kind or nature they may be, in as full and effectual a manner, as any person or persons, bodies corporate, or politic can, or may do, and may have a common seal, and may alter the same at pleasure. The said president and trustees shall require their clerk to keep a fair journal and record of all their proceedings, and record all by-laws and ordinances which they may make, in a book to be provided for that purpose.

Sec. 5 The president and trustees, or a majority of them, of any town incorporated as herein directed, shall have power to make, ordain, and establish and execute such ordinances in writing, not inconsistent with the laws, or the constitution of this state, as they shall deem necessary to prevent and remove nuisances, to restrain and prohibit gambling or other disorderly conduct, and to prevent the running of, and indecent exhibitions of horses, within the bounds of such town; to provide for licensing public shows; to regulate and establish markets; to sink and keep in repair public wells; to keep open and in repair the street and alleys of such town, by making pavements, or sidewalks, as to them may seem needful: provident always that the lot in front of which any sidewalk is made, shall be taxed to pay at least one-half of the expenses of making such sidewalk. The said president and trustees shall also have power to provide such means as they may deem necessary to protect such town from injuries by fires. And for the purpose of carrying the aforesaid powers into effect, the said president and trustees shall have power to define the boundaries of such town; provided, that the same shall not exceed one mile square, and to levy and collect annually a tax, on all the real estate in such town, not exceeding fifty cents on every hundred dollars, of assessment valuation thereof.

Sec. 6 It shall be the duty of the said president and trustees, to cause all the street and alleys of such town, and all the public roads passing from and through such town, for one mile from the center thereof, to be kept in good repair; and to this end, they are authorized to require every male resident of such town, over the age of twenty-one years, to labor in said street, alleys and roads, at least three days in each and every year; and if such labor shall be insufficient, to appropriate so much of the tax levied on real estate, as may be necessary to keep the said street, alleys and roads in repair. . . .

THE CHARTER OF 1835

Two years after its organization, the town of Chicago had its charter changed in order to increase its corporate powers. The reason for the change was the growth of population within the existing boundaries of the town.

(Source: Edmund J. James, The Charters of the City of Chicago, Part I, The Early Charters, 1833-1837. Chicago, 1898.)

(Second Charter of the Town of Chicago, being a special act of the legislature entitled "An Act to change the corporate powers of the Town of Chicago." Passed February 11, 1835. In effect the first Monday in June, 1835.)

Section 1. Be it enacted by the people of the State of Illinois, represented in the General Assembly, That John H. Kinzie, Gurdon S. Hubbard, Ebenezer Goodrich, John K. Boyer, and John S.C. Hogan, be, and they are hereby constituted a body politic and corporate, to be known by the name of the "Trustees of the town of Chicago," and by that name, they, and their successors shall be known in law, have perpetual succession, sue and be sued, implead and be impleaded, defend and be defended in courts of law and equity, and in all actions and matters whatsoever; may grant, purchase, and receive and hold property, real and personal within the said town, and no other, (burial grounds excepted), and may lease, sell, and dispose of the same for the benefit of the town and shall have power to lease any of the reserved lands which have been, or may hereafter be appropriated to the use of said town, and may do all other acts, as natural persons: may have a common seal, and break and alter the same at pleasure.

Sec. 2. That all that district of country contained in sections nine and sixteen, north and south fractional sections ten, and fractional section fifteen, in township thirty-nine north, of range fourteen east, of the third principal meridian, is hereby declared to be within the boundaries of the town of Chicago: Provided, That the authority of the board of trustees of the said town of Chicago, shall not extend over the south fractional section ten until the same shall cease to be occupied by the United States.

Sec. 3. That the corporate powers and duties of said town, shall be vested in nine trustees, (after the term of the present incumbent shall have expired, towit: on the first Monday of June next, and to be chosen and appointed as hereinafter directed), who shall form a board for the transaction of business.

Sec. 4. The members composing the board of trustees, shall be elected annually, on the first Monday in June, by hte persons residing within said town, (qualified to vote for representative to the legislature), to serve for one year; they shall be at least twenty-one years of age, citizens of the United States, and inhabitants of said town, and shall possess a freehold estate within the limits thereof.

Sec. 5. That the board of trustees shall appoint their president from their own body; shall appoint all other officers of their board and shall be the judges of the qualifications, elections, and returns of their own members; a majority shall constitute a board to do business, but a smaller number may adjourn from day to day; may compel the attendance of absent members, in such manner and under such penalties as the board may provide; they may determine the rule of proceeding, and make such other rules and regulations for their own government, as to them may seem proper and expedient.

Sec. 6. That the board of trustees shall have power to levy and collect taxes upon all real estate within the town, not exceeding the one-half of one per centum upon the assessed value thereof, except as hereinafter excepted; to make regulations to secure the general health of the inhabitants; to prevent and remove nuisances; to establish night watches; erect lamps in the streets, and lighting the same; to regulate and license ferries within the corporation; to lease the wharfing privilege of said town, giving to the owner or owners, occupant or occupants of the lots fronting the river, the preference of such privilege; to erect and keep in repair bridges; to provide for licensing, taxing and regulating theatrical and other shows, billiard tables and other amusements; to restrain and prohibit gaming houses, bawdy houses, and other disorderly houses; to build market houses; establish and regulate markets; to open and keep in repair streets, avenues, lanes, alleys, drains and sewers; to keep the same clean and free from incumbrances; to establish and regulate a fire department, and to provide for the prevention and extinguishment of fires; to regulate the storage of gun powder and other combustible materials; to erect pumps and wells in the streets, for the convenience of the inhabitants; to regulate the police of the town; to regulate the election of the town officers; to fix their compensation; to establish and enforce quarantine laws; and from time to time, to pass such ordinances to carry into effect the ordinances of this act, and the powers hereby granted, as the good of the inhabitants may require, and to impose and appropriate fines and forfeitures for the breach of any ordinance, and to provide for the collection thereof: <u>Provided,</u> That said trustees shall, in no case, levy a tax upon lots owned by the state.

Sec. 7. That upon the application of the owners of two-thirds of real estate, on any street or parts of a street, it shall be lawful for the board of trustees to levy and collect a special tax on the owners of the lots on the said street or parts of a street, according to their respective fronts, for the purpose of grading and paving the sidewalks on said street.

Sec. 8. That the board of trustees shall have power to regulate, grade, pave and improve the streets, avenues, lanes and alleys within the limits of said town, and to extend, open and widen the same, making the person or persons injured thereby, adequate compensation. . . .

THE FIRST CITY CHARTER OF CHICAGO - 1837

On March 4, 1837, Chicago was incorporated as a city, and received its first city charter. Its population at the time was only 4,170. A portion of this charter is cited here.

(Source: Edmund J. James, ed., The Charters of the City of Chicago, Part I, The Early Charters, 1833-1837. Chicago, 1898.)

Section 1. Be it enacted by the people of the State of Illinois represented in the General Assembly, That the district of country in the county of Cook in the state aforesaid, known as the east half of the southeast quarter of section thirty-three, in township forty, and fractional section thirty-four in the same township, the east fourth part of sections six, seven, eighteen and nineteen, in the same township, also fractional section three, section four, section five, section eight, section nine, and fractional section ten, excepting the southwest fractional quarter of section ten, occupied as a military post, until the same shall become private property, fractional section fifteen, section sixteen, section seventeen, section twenty, section twenty-one, and fractional section twenty-two, in township thirty-nine north range number fourteen east of the third principal meridian, in the state aforesaid, shall hereafter be known by the name of the city of Chicago.

Sec. 2. The inhabitants of said city, shall be a corporation by the name of the city of Chicago, and may sue and be sued, complain and defend in any court, make and use a common seal, and alter it at pleasure, and take, hold, purchase and convey such real and personal estate, as the purposes of the corporation may require.

Sec. 3. The said city shall be divided into six wards, as follows: All that part of the city which lies south of Chicago river and east of the center of Clark street, following the center of Clark street to the south line of section sixteen, to the center of State street, and all that part of said city which lies east of the center of said State street, and a line parallel with the center of said street, to the southern boundary of said city, shall be denominated the first ward of said city. All that part of said city which lies south of said Chicago river, west of the first ward, and east of the south branch of said Chicago river, shall be denominated the second ward of said city; all that part of said city, lying west of the aforesaid south branch of the said Chicago river, and south of the center of Randolph street, and by a line parallel with the center of said Randolph street, to the western boundary of said city, shall be denominated the third ward; all that part of said city which lies north of the said third ward and west of the said Chicago river, and the north and south branches thereof, shall be denominated the fourth ward of said city; all that part of said city which lies north of the Chicago river, and east of the north branch thereof, and west of the center of Clark street, to the center of Chicago avenue, and lying south of the center of Chicago avenue, to the center of Franklin street, and lying west of Franklin street, and a line parallel with the center thereof, to the northern boundary of said city, shall be denominated the fifth ward; all that part of said city lying north of the Chicago river, and east of the said fifth ward, shall be denominated the sixth ward of said city.

Sec. 4. There shall be in and for the said city, except as hereinafterwards provided, one mayor, twelve aldermen, one clerk, one treasurer, six assessors, one or more collectors, and such other officers as are hereinafter authorized to be appointed, which with said mayor, aldermen, and assessors, shall be free holders in the said city.

Sec. 5. An election shall be held in each of the wards of said city, on the first Tuesday in March in each year, after the year eighteen hundred and thirty-seven, at such place as the common council of said city may appoint, and of which six days previous public notice shall be given in writing, in three public places in each ward by the inspectors thereof.

Sec. 6. At the first election under this act, and at each annual election thereafter, there shall be elected two aldermen and one assessor from each ward, each of whom shall be an actual resident of the ward in which he was elected, <u>Provided however</u>, That the aforesaid wards, denominated the third and fifth wards, shall be entitled to elect but one alderman for each ward, until the annual election for the year <u>anno domini</u> 1839.

Sec. 7. The common council shall appoint three inspectors of elections for each ward, who shall be inspectors of elections after the first. Such inspectors shall have the same power and authority as the inspectors of a general state election.

Sec. 8. The manner of conducting and voting at the elections to be held under this act, and the keeping of the poll lists thereof, shall be the same, as nearly as may be, as is provided by law, at the general state election, <u>Provided</u>, That the common council may hereafter, if expedient, change the mode of election to that by ballot, and prescribe the manner of conduction the same.

Sec. 9. Every person voting at such election, shall be an actual resident of the ward in which he so votes, shall be a house holder within the city, or shall have paid a city tax of not less than three dollars, within twelve months next preceding such election, and shall have resided in said city at least six months next preceding such election, and shall moreover if required by any person qualified to vote thereat, before he is permitted to vote, take the following oath: you swear or affirm that you are of the age of twenty-one years, that you have been a resident of this city for six months immediately preceding this election, that you are a house holder therein, or that you have paid a city tax of not less than three dollars within twelve months next preceding this election, and that you are now a resident of this ward, and have not voted at this election. . . .

THE CHICAGO CONSOLIDATION ACT - 1851

In 1851, Chicago received its second city charter from the State Legislature. Its purpose was to consolidate all the laws incorporating the city of Chicago, into one new charter, a part of which f follows.

(Source: Edmund J. James, <u>The Charters of the City of Chicago,</u> Part II <u>The City Charters, 1838-1851.</u> Chicago, 1899.)

<u>Be it enacted by the people of the State of Illinois represented in the General Assembly</u>:
 I. That the district of country in the county of Cook and state of Illinois, known and described as follows, to-wit: all that part of township thirty-nine north, range fourteen east of the third principal meridian, which lies north of the north line of sections twenty-seven, twenty-eight, twenty-nine, and thirty of said township, and the east half of section thirty-three, and fractional section thirty-four in township forty north, range fourteen east, is hereby erected into a city by the name of the <u>City of Chicago.</u>
 II. The inhabitants of said city shall be a corporation by the name of the City of Chicago; and by that name sue and be sued, complain and defend in any court; make and use a common seal and alter it at pleasure, and take, hold, and purchase, lease and convey, such real and personal or mixed estate as the purposes of the corporation may require, within or without the limits aforesaid.
 III. The city of Chicago shall be divided into nine wards, as follows:
 <u>First ward</u>. All that part of the city which lies south of the center of Chicago river, and east of the center of State street, and a line running due south from the center of the last named street, shall be denominated the first ward.
 <u>Second ward</u>. All that part of said city which lies south of the center of said Chicago river, west of the first ward, and east of the center of Clark street, and a line running due south from the center of the last named street, shall be denominated the second ward.
 <u>Third ward</u>. All that part of said city which lies south of the center of said Chicago river, west of the second ward, and east of the center of Wells street, and a line running due south from the center of the last named street, shall be denominated the third ward.
 <u>Fourth ward</u>. All that part of said city which lies south of the center of the said Chicago river, west of the third ward, and east of the center of the south branch of the Chicago river, shall be denominated the fourth ward.

Fifth ward. All that part of said city which lies west of the center of the south branch of Chicago river, and south of the center of Randolph street, and a line running due west from the center of the last named street, shall be denominated the fifth ward.

Sixth ward. All that part of said city lying west of the center of Chicago river, and north and south branches thereof, and north of the center of Randolph street, and a line running due west from the center of the last named street, shall be denominated the sixth ward.

Seventh ward. All that part of said city which lies east of the center of the north branch of the Chicago river, and north of the center of the Chicago river, and west of the center of La Salle street, and a line running due north from the center of the last named street, shall be denominated the seventh ward.

Eighth ward. All that part of said city which lies north of the center of the Chicago river, and east of the seventh ward, and west of the center of Wolcott street, and a line running due north from the center of the last named street, shall be denominated the eighth ward.

Ninth ward. All that part of said city which lies north of the center of the Chicago river, east of Wolcott street, and a line running due north from the center of the last named street, shall be denominated the ninth ward ....

THE CITY CHARTER OF 1863

By the early 1860's, Chicago's growth had been phenomenal. She was no longer a small midwestern city, but, rather a budding metropolis. As a result, it became necessary to revise her charter, so as to provide more authority for the municipality. A portion of the new charter follows.

(Source: Charter of the City of Chicago, February 13, 1863.)

1. CORPORATE POWERS.] Act February 13, 1863. SECTION 1. The inhabitants of all that district of country in the county of Cook and state of Illinois, contained within the limits and boundaries hereinafter prescribed, shall be a body politic under the name and style of the City of Chicago; and by that name sue and be sued, complain and defend, in any court; make and use a common seal, and alter it at pleasure; and take and hold, purchase, lease and convey such real and personal or mixed estate as the purposes of the corporation may require, within or without the limits aforesaid.

2. CORPORATE LIMITS.] Ibid. SEC. 2. The corporate limits and jurisdiction of the city of Chicago shall embrace and include, within the same, all of township thirty-nine north, range fourteen east of the third principal meridian, and all of sections thirty-one, thirty-two, thirty-three and fractional section thirty-four, in township forty, north, range fourteen, east of the third principal meridian, together with so much of the waters and bed of Lake Michigan as lies within one mile of the shore thereof and east of the territory aforesaid.

3. DIVISIONS -- NORTH, SOUTH, WEST -- LIMITS OF.] Ibid. SEC. 3. All that portion of the aforesaid territory lying north of the center of the main Chicago river and east of the center of the north branch of said river, shall constitute the North Division of said city; all that portion of the aforesaid territory lying south of the center of the main Chicago river and south and east of the center of the south branch of said river and of the Illinois and Michigan canal, shall constitute the South Division of said city; and all that portion of the aforesaid territory lying west of the center of the north and south branches of said river and of the Illinois and Michigan canal, shall constitute the West Division of said city........

THE FIRE DEPARTMENT - 1863

Although a fire department was established for the city in 1854, it proved quite inefficient. As a result, in 1863, the organization and operations of this department were revised and expanded as part of the new City Charter of 1863. A portion of that section of the charter pertaining to the improved fire department follows.

(Source: Charter of the City of Chicago, February 13, 1863.)

1. POWER TO PRESCRIBE FIRE LIMITS.] Act February 13, 1863, chap. 12. SECTION 1. The common council, for the purpose of guarding against the calamities of fire, shall have power to prescribe the limits within which wooden buildings shall not be erected or placed or repaired without permission, and to direct that all and any buildings, within the limits prescribed, shall be made or constructed of fire-proof materials, and to prohibit the repairing or rebuilding of wooden buildings, within the fire limits, when the same shall have been damaged to the extent of fifty per cent of the value thereof, and to prescribe the manner of ascertaining such damage.

2. GENERAL POWER OF COUNCIL AS TO FIRES -- CHIMNEYS -- MANUFACTORIES, ETC.] Ibid. SEC. 2. The common council shall also have power:

First. To prevent the dangerous construction and condition of chimneys, fire-places, hearths, stoves, stove pipes, ovens, boilers and apparatus used in and about any building or manufactory, and to cause the same to be removed or placed in a safe and secure condition, when considered dangerous.

Second. To prevent the deposit of ashes in unsafe places, and to cause all such buildings and enclosures as may be in a dangerous state, to be put in safe condition.

Third. To regulate and prevent the carrying on of manufactories dangerous in causing or promoting fire.

Fourth. To regulate and prevent the use of fire-works and fire-arms.

Fifth. To compel the owners or occupants of houses or other buildings, to have scuttles in the roofs, and stairs or ladders leading to the same.

Sixth. To authorize the mayor, aldermen, police, or other officers of said city, to keep away from the vicinity of any fire all idle and suspicious persons and to compel all officers of said city, and other persons, to aid in the extinguishment of fires, and in the preservation of property exposed to danger thereat.

Seventh. And, generally, to establish such regulations, for the prevention and extinguishment of fires, as the common council may deem expedient.

3. ALDERMEN AND FIREMEN EXEMPT FROM JURY DUTY.] Ibid. SEC. 7. The members of the common council and firemen shall, during their term of service as such, be exempt from serving on juries in all courts of this state, and in the militia. The name of each fireman shall be registered with the clerk of the city, and the evidence to entitle him to the exemption provided in this section shall be the certificate of the clerk, made within the year in which the exemption is claimed.

4. FUND TO BE SET APART FOR RELIEF OF DISABLED FIREMEN.] Ibid. SEC. 8. One-eighth part of the amount of all fire insurance rates which shall be annually paid into the city treasury, as hereinbefore provided, shall be reserved and set apart, to create a fund for the relief of distressed firemen who may become disabled in the service of the city; and shall be used solely for that purpose. Said money shall be disbursed in such sums, and under such rules and regulations, as the common council shall prescribe. The remaining seven-eights of the aforesaid revenue shall be retained by the city and allowed to accumulate, until a sufficient sum shall have been realized to defray the expense of establishing a fire alarm or fire telegraph system in said city, and shall be then used for that purpose. After this purpose shall have been accomplished, this portion of the aforesaid revenue shall be applied to the purchase of fire engines and other apparatus used for the extinguishment of fires.

5. BOARD OF POLICE TO CONTROL FIRE DEPARTMENT.] SEC. 23. The board of police of said city shall assume and exercise the entire control of the fire department of said city, and shall possess full power and authority over its organization, government, appointments and discipline, within said city. It shall have the custody and control of the engine-houses, engines, hose carts, trucks, ladders, horses, telegraph lines, and all other public property and equipments belonging to the fire department.

6. ORGANIZATION OF FIRE DEPARTMENT.] Ibid. SEC. 24. The fire department of said city shall consist of a fire marshal and assistant marshals, not exceeding three, and as many competent, able and respectable citizens of said city as shall be appointed by the board, to be known as the fire police, who shall, under the direction of said board, have the care and management of the engines, apparatus, equipments, engine-house, and other property used and provided for the extinguishment of fires: Provided, that the common council may limit the number of the fire police. The said offices of marshal and fire police, hereby created, shall be severally filled by the appointment of said board. It shall promulgate all regulations and orders relating to the fire department through the fire marshal, and it shall be the duty of the subordinate officers and the fire police, to respect and obey the said marshal as the head and chief of the department, subject to the rules, regulations and general orders of the board. . . .

THE BOARD OF HEALTH - 1867

In March, 1867, the Illinois State Legislature permitted the City Council of Chicago to establish its first official Board of Health. A portion of this act follows.

(Source: Laws of the State of Illinois, Chicago, 1867.)

1. BOARD OF HEALTH, HOW CONSTITUTED.] Act March 9, 1867, chap. 4. SECTION 1. The mayor of the city of Chicago, with six other persons, to be appointed on the passage of this act by the judges of the superior court of Chicago, each of whom shall be a resident of said city, and three of whom, and no more, shall be physicians, shall constitute the board of health of the city of Chicago. Said board of health shall have, and there is hereby conferred on said board, such powers and duties as may be necessary to promote or preserve the safety or health of the city, or improve its sanitary condition.

2. POWERS OF.] Ibid. SEC. 2. Said board of health may enact such by-laws, rules and regulations as it may deem advisable, in harmony with the provisions and objects of this act and all acts, the object of which is to promote and preserve the health, safety and sanitary condition of the city, now existing or that may hereafter be passed, not inconsistent with the constitution or laws of this state, for the regulation of the action of said board, its officers and agents, in the discharge of its and their duties, and for the regulation of the citizens or public, and, from time to time, may alter, amend or annul the same.

3. TERM OF MEMBERS -- OATH -- BONDS.] Ibid. SEC. 3. The six members appointed, as herein provided, shall be divided into three classes; the first class shall hold office for two years; the second class for four years, and the third class for six years; and they shall determine by lot at the first meeting of said board which two of them shall hold office for the respective terms of two years, four and six years. Vacancies occurring in the said board, by the expiration of the term of office of either class, shall be filled by appointment by the judges of the superior court of Chicago for six years; any vacancy caused by either removal, resignation or death, shall be filled in like manner for the unexpired term. The members of said board, appointed as herein provided, shall receive an annual salary of not less than five hundred dollars, to be fixed by the common council. Before entering upon the duties of their office, they shall take the oath prescribed for state officers in the constitution of the state, and they shall also give bonds to the said city in the sum of twenty-five thousand dollars each, conditioned for the faithful performance of their duties as members of the board of health under the provisions of this act, said bonds to be ap-

proved by the judges of the superior court of Chicago, and filed with their oath of office in the office of the city clerk. And in case of failure to comply with the requirements of this section, prior to the first meeting of said board, the office of such member, so failing to take the prescribed oath and give a bond, shall be deemed vacant, and shall be filled as in this act provided. The members of the board of health may be removed from office for like cause and in like manner as the board of police or the members of the board of public works.

4. TO REPORT, ANNUALLY, CONDITION AND EXPENDITURES OF DEPARTMENT.] Ibid. SEC. 4. It shall be the duty of the board of health, on or before the first Monday in April of each year, to report in writing the condition of the health department, and a statement of the expenditures of the health board for the year, to the common council.

5. PRESIDENT -- SECRETARY -- DUTIES OF.] Ibid. SEC. 5. The said board of health shall meet at the office of the mayor of the city of Chicago, on or before the first Monday of April next, and organize by the election of one of their number president, and by appointing a competent person to be secretary of said board, and the successive presidents of said board of health shall be annually elected from the members thereof. The secretary shall keep a correct and complete record of all the acts, doings and proceedings of said board; he shall receive an annual salary to be fixed by the board and shall hold office during the pleasure of said board, but but shall not be a member thereof.

6. SANITARY SUPERINTENDENT TO BE APPOINTED -- SALARY OF.] Act March 10, 1869. SEC. 14. The board of health are hereby authorized and required to select from their number one who shall act as sanitary superintendent, and who shall devote his whole time to the duties of said office for which he is to receive, in addition to his salary as commissioner, the sum of twenty-five hundred dollars, payable at such times and in such manner as the salary of commissioner is now paid.

7. POLICE PATROLMENT MAY BE APPOINTED ON SANITARY SQUAD.] Act March 9, 1867, chap. 4. SEC. 6. The board of police shall appoint such additional police patrolmen, to be subject to the rules and regulations of the police department, as the board of health may, from time to time, in writing, request, to be detailed as a sanitary squad and be paid out of the health fund, the length of time for which they are wanted to be stated in said written request.

8. ANNUAL ESTIMATE OF EXPENSE TO BE SUBMITTED -- TAX FOR -- WARRANTS.] Ibid. SEC. 7. It shall be the duty of the board of health to prepare and submit to the comptroller, on or before the first day of May in every year, an estimate of the whole cost and expenses of providing for and maintaining the health department of said city during the current fiscal year, which estimate shall be laid, by said comptroller, before the common council with his annual estimate. The common council may provide for the amount so required in the general tax levy to be laid on said city. Said money shall be paid into the city treasury. . . .

THE CHARTER OF 1870

A number of Amendments were added to the charter of 1863, and incorporated into a revised charter in 1870. The portion of the new charter that follows deals with the new ward organization for the city.

(Source: <u>Charter of the City of Chicago</u>, Chicago, 1870.)

4. BOUNDARIES EXTENDED.] SEC. 1. That the territorial limits of the city of Chicago, shall be and are hereby extended as follows: That part of section thirty (30), township forty (40), north of range fourteen (14) east of the third (3d) principal meridian, which lies west of the north branch of the Chicago river; section twenty-five (25), township forty (40) north of range thirteen (13) east of the third (3d) principal meridian, except that part of said section lying east of the center of the north branch of the Chicago river; sections twenty-six (26), thirty-five (35), and thirty-six (36) in township forty (40) north of range thirteen (13) east of the third (3d) principal meridian; sections one (1), two (2), eleven (11), twelve (12), thirteen (13), fourteen (14), twenty-three (23), twenty-four (24), twenty-five (25) and twenty-six (26) in township thirty-nine (39) north of range thirteen (13) east of the third (3d) principal meridian; and that part of section thirty-five (35) and thirty-six (36) in township thirty-nine (39) north of range thirteen (13) east of the third (3d) principal meridian, lying northwest of the center of the Illinois and Michigan canal, shall be and are hereby added to said city, and shall constitute a part of the west division of said city and of the town of West Chicago; and the said added or new territory shall cease to be a part of the several towns to which it now belongs or appertains; and the outside boundary of the west division of the city of Chicago as hereby established, shall be the outside boundary of the several wards of said city which now extend to the present city limits.

5. TERRITORY EXCEPTED.] SEC. 1 That the act entitled "An act to amend the charter of the city of Chicago, to create a board of park commissioners and authorize a tax in the town of West Chicago and for other purposes." ... including the affirmance of the propositions specified in the first clause of the twentieth section of said act, but excluding the remainder of said section, relating to the holding of an election now past, shall be and is hereby re-enacted and confirmed, and shall be in full force and effect to all intents and purposes, except as hereinafter specified: <u>Provided</u>, that the four added sections of land from the town of Jefferson in said act specified, viz.: section twenty-five (25), twenty-six (26), thirty-five (35) and thirty-six (36) in township forty (40) north of range thirteen (13) east, shall not become a part of the city of Chicago, or of the town of West Chi-

cago; nor shall the jurisdiction of said city be extended over the same, but the same shall remain a part of the town of Jefferson, the same as if the act had not been passed.

6. WARD BOUNDARIES.] ... SEC. 4. The city of Chicago shall be divided into twenty wards, as follows:

First ward. All that part of the south division of said city which lies south of the center of the main Chicago river and north of the center of Monroe street shall be denominated the first ward.

Second ward. All that part of the south division of said city which lies south of the center of Monroe street and north of the center of Harrison street shall be denominated the second ward.

Third ward. All that part of the south division of said city which lies south of the center of Harrison street and north of the center of Sixteenth street shall be denominated the third ward.

Fourth ward. All that part of the south division of said city, which lies south of the center of Sixteenth street and east of the center of Clark street, and a line corresponding with the center of the named street projected southerly to the center of Twenty-sixth street and north of the center of said Twenty-sixth street, and a line corresponding with the center of the last named street projected easterly to Lake Michigan, shall be denominated the fourth ward.

Fifth ward. All that part of the south division of said city which lies south of the center of Twenty-sixth street and a line corresponding with the center of said street projected easterly to Lake Michigan, and east of the center of Clark street and a line corresponding with the center of the last named street projected southerly to the city limits, shall be denominated the fifth ward.

Sixth ward. All that part of the south division of said city which lies south of the center of Sixteenth street and west of the center of Clark street, and a line corresponding with the center of the last named street projected southerly to the city limits, shall be denominated the sixth ward.

Seventh ward. All that part of the west division of said city which lies south of the center of Sixteenth street shall be denominated the seventh ward.

Eighth ward. All that part of the west division of said city which lies north of the center of Sixteenth street and south of the center of Twelfth street shall be denominated the eighth ward.

Ninth ward. All that portion of the west division of said city which lies north of the center of Twelfth street, east of the center of Center avenue and south of the center of Van Buren street shall be denominated the ninth ward.

Tenth ward. All that part of the west division of said city which lies north of the center of Van Buren street, east of the center of Aberdeen and Curtis streets and south of the center of Randolph street shall be denominated the tenth ward.

Eleventh ward. All that part of the west division of said city which lies north of the center of Randolph street, east of the center of Curtis street and south of the center of Fourth street shall be denominated the eleventh ward.

Twelfth ward. All that part of the west division of said city which lies north of the center of Twelfth street, east of the center of Reuben street, south of the center of Fourth street and west of the following boundary, viz.: commencing at the center of Fourth street and running thence south on the center of Curtis and Aberdeen streets to the center of Van Buren street, thence west on the center of Van Buren street to the center of Center avenue, thence south on the center of Center avenue to the center of Twelfth street shall be denominated the twelfth ward.

Thirteenth ward. All that part of the west division of said city which lies north of the center of Twelfth street, west of the center of Reuben street and south of the center of Lake street shall be denominated the thirteenth ward.

Fourteenth ward. All that part of the west division of said city which lies north of the center of Lake street, south of the center of Chicago avenue and west of the center of Reuben street shall be denominated the fourteenth ward.

Fifteenth ward. All that part of the west division of said city which lies north of the center of Fourth street and Chicago avenue, not included in any of the foregoing wards, shall be denominated the fifteenth ward.

Sixteenth ward. All that part of the north division of said city which lies north of the center of North avenue shall be denominated the sixteenth ward.

Seventeenth ward. All that part of the north division of said city which lies south of the center of North avenue and north of the center of Division street shall be denominated the seventeenth ward.

Eighteenth ward. All that part of the north division of said city which lies south of the center of Division street and west of the center of Franklin street shall be denominated the eighteenth ward.

Nineteenth ward. All that part of the north division of said city which lies south of the center of Division street, east of the center of Franklin street and north of the center of Chicago avenue shall be denominated the nineteenth ward.

Twentieth ward. All that part of the north division of said city which lies south of the center of Chicago avenue and east of the center of Franklin street shall be denominated the twentieth ward.

7. CHANGE OF WARD BOUNDARIES.] Act March 11, 1869. SEC. 2. That the act passed by the present general assembly, prescribing and defining the boundaries of the wards in said city and for other purposes, be, and the same is hereby, so amended that the north and south boundaries of the ninth ward, created under said act, be, and the same are hereby, extended westwardly to the center of Loomis street, and the center of the last named street shall be the western boundary thereof, and also the eastern boundary of the twelfth ward, as established by said act, south of the center of Van Buren street....

THE GREAT CHICAGO FIRE - 1871

On the night of October 8, 1871, a great fire engulfed large sections of Chicago. The blaze burned all the next day, doing considerable damage and taking scores of lives. The following selection is part of the official proclamations, orders and correspondence of R. B. Mason, the mayor of Chicago, concerned with this catastrophe.

(Source: <u>Proclamations, Orders and Correspondence, Chicago Mayor</u>, October, 1871.)

WHEREAS, in the Providence of God, to whose will we humbly submit, a terrible calamity has befallen our city, which demands of us our best efforts for the preservation of order, and the relief of the suffering;

BE IT KNOWN that the faith and credit of the city of Chicago is hereby pledged for the necessary expenses for the relief of the suffering. Public order will be preserved. The Police and Special Police now being appointed, will be responsible for the maintenance of the peace and the protection of property. All officers and men of the Fire Department and Health Department will act as Special Policemen without further notice. The Mayor and Comptroller will give vouchers for all supplies furnished by the different Relief Committees. The head-quarters of the City Government will be at the Congregational Church, corner of West Washington and Ann Sts. All persons are warned against any acts tending to endanger property. All persons caught in any depredation will be immediately arrested.

With the help of God, order and peace and private property shall be preserved. The City Government and committees of citizens pledge themselves to the community to protect them, and prepare the way for a restoration of public and private welfare.

It is believed the fire has spent its force, and all will soon be well.

R.B. MASON, <u>Mayor</u>
GEO. TAYLOR, <u>Comptroller</u>.
CHAS. C.P. HOLDEN, <u>President Common Council</u>.
T.B. BROWN, <u>President Board of Police</u>.
CHICAGO, <u>October 9th</u>, 1871.

CHICAGO, October 10, 1871.

The following Ordinance was passed at a meeting of the Common Council of the City of Chicago, on the 10th day of October, A.D. 1871:

An Ordinance

Be it ordained by the Common Council of the City of Chicago:

SECTION 1. -- That the Price of Bread in the City of Chicago for the next 10 days is hereby fixed and established at <u>Eight</u> (8) <u>Cents per Loaf</u> of 12 ounces, and at the same rate for all Loaves of less or greater weight.

SECTION 2. -- Any person selling or attempting to sell any bread within the City of Chicago, within said 10 days, at a greater price than is fixed in this Ordinance, shall be liable to a penalty of ten (10) dollars for each and every offense, to be collected as other penalties for violation of City Ordinances.

SECTION 3. -- This Ordinance shall be in full force and effect from and after its passage.

<u>Approved</u> October 10th, 1871.

Attest: R.B. MASON, Mayor.

N. [C.T.] HOTCHKISS, <u>City Clerk</u>

1. All citizens are requested to exercise great caution in the use of fire in their dwellings, and not to use kerosene lights at present, as the city will be without a full supply of water for probably two or three days.

2. The following bridges are passable, to-wit: All bridges (except Van Buren and Adams Streets) from Lake Street south, and all bridges over the North Branch of the Chicago River.

3. All good citizens who are willing to serve are requested to report at the corner of Ann and Washington Streets, to be sworn in as special policemen.

Citizens are requested to organize a police for each block in the city, and to send reports of such organization to the police head-quarters, corner of Union and West Madison Streets.

All persons needing food will be relieved by applying at the following places:

At the corner of Ann and Washington; Illinois Central Railroad roundhouse.

M.S.R.R. -- Twenty-second Street Station.

C.B. & Q.R.R. -- Canal Street Depot.

St. L. & A.R.R. -- Near Sixteenth Street.

C. & N.W.R.R. -- Corner of Kinzie and Canal Streets.

All the public school-houses, and at nearly all the churches.

4. Citizens are requested to avoid passing through the burnt districts until the dangerous walls left standing can be leveled.

5. All saloons are ordered to be closed by 8 P.M. every day for one week, under a penalty of forfeiture of license.

6. The Common Council have this day, by ordinance, fixed the price of bread at <u>eight</u> (8) <u>cents</u> per loaf of 12 ounces, and at the same rate for loaves of a greater or less weight, and affixed a penalty of ten dollars for selling or attempting to sell, bread at a greater rate within the next ten days. . . .

A BUILDING CONSTRUCTION ORDINANCE - 1872

Following the disastrous Chicago fire, the City Council passed an ordinance which outlawed the construction of wooden buildings in the downtown area, as well as defined other fire prevention measures.

(Source: Journal of the City Council of Chicago, Chicago, 1873.)

Be it ordained by the Common Council of the city of Chicago.
SECTION 1. The present and future limits of the City of Chicago shall be the "fire limits" of said city and no building shall hereafter be erected within the limits of said city unless the roof, the outsides party and division walls shall be constructed of non-cumbustible materials; nor shall any wooden building within the said city, when the same shall have been damaged to the extent of 50 percent of its value, be repaired or rebuilt; the extent of such damage to be ascertained in the manner provided by this ordinance; nor shall any building be hereafter erected in said city, unless a permit for the erection thereof shall have first been obtained from the Board of Public Works of said city: Provided, however, the fee for the issuing of any such permit shall not exceed fifty cents.
SECTION 2. No building or structure of any kind or description shall be erected, constructed, or repaired within the city limits, as described in section one of this ordinance, unless the same be done with brick, stone, iron, or other incombustible materials, and all buildings which shall, or may hereafter, be erected, or constructed within the said city limits shall have outside walls of not less than one foot in thickness: and if any such building shall be more than two and not more than three stories in height (above the basement), the outside and party walls of the basement and first story shall be not less than sixteen inches in thickness; and if any such building shall be more than three stories in height (above the basement); the outside walls of the basement and first story shall not be less than sixteen and the party walls not less than twenty inches thickness; the outside walls of the second and third stories shall not be less than twelve inches in thickness, and the party walls not less than sixteen inches, and the walls of the remaining stories not less than twelve inches in thickness: Provided, however, that when any building of more than three stories in height (above basement) is to be erected, the lateral outside wall of which is to be built adjoining or within less than four inches of the lateral outside wall of any building already erected, then the first mentioned wall, as to the first, second, and third stories, may not be less than sixteen inches in thickness: and provided further, that buildings erected and used as dwellings only may be constructed with walls in all cases, four inches less

in thickness than is above specified. No building which may be erected shall have any bay or oriel window constructed of wood extending over three feet above the floor of the third story of said building, and no cornice constructed of wood shall be allowed on any building over two stories in height, counting the basement as one story, and no felt, tar or composite roofing of of any kind shall be placed upon or used in the construction of the roof of any building with the said city limits, except the same is laid upon or over a coat of water lime cement of not less than one-half inch in thickness. The felt must be covered with distilled cement (and the use of crude coal tar or crude pine tar for this purpose is prohibited), and well-covered with gravel. If a French or Mansard roof be placed upon any building, the same shall be constructed of fire-proof material. Whenever two or more buildings, which may hereafter be constructed within the city limits, shall be so built that their walls shall come together or touch each other, there shall be erected and maintained between such buildings, for the entire depth there of, a fire or partition wall of brick, which said wall shall not be less than one foot in thickness, and at least eighteen inches in height above the roofs of such buildings; and all outside and party walls shall be carried up not less than eighteen inches above the roof of any such building. All posts, beams, and other timbers in outside and party walls of buildings in said city limits shall be separated at least eight inches from each other, with stone or brick, laid in mortar or cement. There shall not be more than thirty feet space between, the party or outside walls of any buildings which may be erected within said city limits, unless such buildings shall be supported by iron or other columns or support of fire-proof material.

SEC. 3. That no building within said limits not constructed and built as provided in section two of this ordinance shall hereafter be occupied or used in whole or in part, as or for any of the trades, occupations or businesses hereinafter mentioned, to the Planing mills, sash, door or blind factories, furniture factory, distillery, brewery, agricultural implements, or wood or willow-ware manufactory, match or fire work manufactory, or the making, distilling, or manufacture of varnish, naptha, coal or other inflammable oil, or alcoholic spirits: nor shall any such trade, occupation, or business be carried on within any building or place in said city without a permit in writing first designed from the Board of Public Works of said city; but it is hereby provided that the said Board of Public Works shall be and are hereby authorized to grant permits for the carrying on of any such trade or occupation or business in any building in said city, which at the time of the passage of this ordinance shall have been occupied or used, in whole or in part, for any such trade, occupation, or business, but upon such terms and conditions as to the using of precautions against fire, as to the removing or storage of material or shavings, as to the inclosing the building with brick, and as to the erection of fire or partition walls in or through any such building, as to the said Board of Public Works may seem proper. All permits issued under this section shall run for one year, but may be renewed annually. Any such permit may be revoked or annulled . . . .

THE ILLINOIS GENERAL CHARTER ACT - 1872

In 1872, the State Legislature passed an act to provide for the incorporation of cities, towns, and villages. Chicago, the largest city in the state by this time, was to operate under this new type of charter, a portion of which follows.

(Source: Laws of the State of Illinois, 27th Session, General Assembly, 1872-72.)

SECTION 1. [OF THE ORGANIZATION OF CITIES.] Be it enacted by the People of the State of Illinois, represented in the General Assembly, as follows: That any city now existing in this state may become incorporated under this act in manner following: Whenever one-eighth of the legal voters of such city voting at the last preceding municipal election shall petition the mayor and council thereof to submit the question as to whether such city shall become incorporated under this act, to a vote of the electors in such city, it shall be the duty of such mayor and council to submit such question accordingly, and to appoint a time and place, or places, at which such vote may be taken, and to designate the persons who shall act as judges at such election. But such question shall not be submitted oftener than once in four years.

§ 2. The mayor of such city shall give at least thirty days notice of such election, by publishing a notice thereof in one or more newspapers within such city; but if no newspaper is published therein, then by posting at least five copies of such notice in each ward.

§ 3. The ballots to be used at such election shall be in the following form: "For city organization under general law;" or, "Against city organization under general law." The judges of such election shall make returns thereof to the city council, whose duty it shall be to canvass such returns and cause the result of such canvass to be entered upon the records of such city. If a majority of the votes cast at such election shall be for city organization under general law, such city shall thenceforth be deemed to be organized under this act; and the city officers then in office shall thereupon exercise the powers conferred upon like officers in this act, until their successors shall be elected and qualified.

§ 4. Any incorporated town in this state, having a population of not less than one thousand inhabitants, may become incorporated as a city in like manner as hereinbefore provided; but in all such cases the president and trustees of such town shall, respectively, perform the same duties relative to such a change of organization as is above required to be performed by the mayor and council of cities.

§ 5. Whenever any area of continuous territory in this state, not exceeding four square miles, shall have resident thereon a population of not less than one thousand inhabitants, which shall not already be included within any incorporated town or city, the same may become incorporated as a city in manner following: Any fifty legal voters thereof may file in the office of the clerk of the county court of the county in which such inhabitants reside, a petition, addressed to the judge of such court; and if the territory described in said petition shall be in more than one county, then the petition shall be addressed to the judge of the court where a great part of such territory is situated -- which petition shall define the boundaries of such proposed city, and state the number of inhabitants residing within such limits, and also state the name of such propsed city, and shall contain a prayer that the question be submitted to the legal voters residing within such limits, whether they will organize as a city under this act. It shall be the duty of the county judge to fix a time and place, within the boundaries of such proposed city, at which an election may be held to determine such question; and such judge shall name the person to act as judges in holding such election, and shall give notice thereof by causing ten notices to be posted in public places within such proposed city. And the third section of this article shall be applicable to such election: <u>Provided,</u> that the returns of such election shall be made to and canvassed by the county judge and any two justices of the peace whom he shall call to his assistance, instead of the city council; and the result of such election shall be entered upon the records of such county court. If a majority of the votes cast at such election shall be "For city organization under general law," the inhabitants of such territory, described in such petition, shall be deemed to be incorporated as a city, under this act, and with the name stated in the petition.

§ 6. All courts in this state shall take judicial notice of the existence of all villages and cities organized under this act, and of the change of the organization of any town or city from its original organization to its organization under this act; and from the time of such organization, or change of organization, the provisions of this act shall be applicable to such cities and villages, and all laws in conflict therewith shall no longer be applicable. But all laws or parts of laws not inconsistent with the provisions of this act, shall continue in force,and applicable to any such city or village, the same as if such change of organization had not taken place.

§ 7. It shall be the duty of the president and board of trustees of any town which shall have voted to change its organization to a city, under this act, to call and give notice of an election to elect city officers, and to designate the time and place or places of holding the same. Such notice shall be published in a newspaper, if there be one, within the town, or posted in ten public places, for at least twenty days before such election. Such president and trustees shall appoint the judges and clerks to hold such election, canvass the returns thereof, and cause the result to be entered upon the records of the town; and the provisions of this act, relative to the elction of city officers, shall be applicable thereto; but, at such election, aldermen may be elected on a general ticket. . . .

CHICAGO SUBURBS - 1873

As early as the 1870's, residents of Chicago began moving out of the city and into suburban areas. This movement was symptomatic of all of urban America during the second half of the nineteenth century.

(Source: Chicago Sunday Times, May 4, 1873.)

Chicago, for its size, is more given to suburbs than any other city in the world. In fact, it is doubtful if any city, of any size, can boast of an equal number of suburban appendages. They are of various population, all the way from 10,000 down to the solitary man who dances attendance on the train at the depot. But all have names, and the enterprising "platter" would be highly indignant if his embryo city were omitted from this list. The number of suburbs of all sorts contiguous to Chicago is nearly a hundred, and they aggregate a population of 50,000 or more, represented by 5,000 or 6,000 heads of families, all of whom do business in the city, and form a large per cent. of the passenger list of the 100 or more trains that enter and leave the city daily.

Chicago, as most people are aware, is situated on an open prairie, skirted on the east by a lake. In the latter direction, therefore, the enterprising real-estate dealer meets with some difficulty in disposing of water-lots, but westward there is an unlimited space, bounded only by the swamps of the Calumet, the Mississippi, the British provinces, and the imagination. Some day the Queen's dominions will be annexed, and then there will be absolutely no limit to Chicago enterprise. At present the real-estate dealer's horizon is bounded by a semi circle radiating about thirty miles from the courthouse. The Sunday Times reporter, who has been devoting himself to this subject for a week or two past, has not yet completed his computation -- he has not yet ascertained the exact number of millions of corner lots within the radius described, to say nothing of the inside lots; but in a rough way, taking the city of London as a divisor, he makes out room enough for a good dozen of such three million and a half hamlets. This may strike the uninitiated reader as a large figure, but those acquainted with Chicago's prospects, and the wonderful elasticity of the suburban property-owner's mind will see nothing surprising in this calculation. Chicago is bound to be the world's city. This is a progressive age, and while the old fogy past has been able to build up a London, what may not be in store for the great city of the future? A hundred years hence this "great and glorious" country will contain a population of 200,000,000 souls. England at present is rated at about 19,000,000 . . .

THE HAYMARKET AFFAIR - 1886

On May 4, 1886, a peaceful rally was held in Chicago's Haymarket Square by a group of Anarcho-Communists. When Chicago police attempted to break up the meeting, someone threw a bomb into their first rank. The police then opened fire on the crowd. Seven policemen were killed, and seventy persons were injured. The following selection describes this event.

(Source: <u>New York Times</u>, May 5, 1886.)

Chicago, May 4. - The villainous teachings of the Anarchists bore bloody fruit in Chicago tonight, and before daylight at least a dozen stalwart men will have laid down their lives as a tribute to the doctrine of Herr Johann Most. There had been skirmishes all day between the police and various sections of the mob, which had no head and no organization. In every instance the police won. In the afternoon a handbill, printed in German and English, called upon "workingmen" to meet at Des Plaines and Randolph streets this evening. "Good speakers," it was promised, "will be present to denounce the latest atrocious act of the police -- the shooting of our fellow-workmen yesterday afternoon."

In response to this invitation 1,400 men, including those most active in the Anarchist riots of the past 48 hours, gathered at the point designated. At Des Plaines-street, Randolph-street, which runs east and west, widens out, and is known as the Old Haymarket. The plaza thus formed is about 2,900 feet long and 150 feet wide. It was just off the northeastern corner of this plaza and around the corner into Des Plaines-street, 100 feet north of Randolph, that the crowd gathered. A light rainstorm came up and about 800 people went away. The 600 who remained listened to speeches from the lips of August Spies, the editor of the <u>Arbiter Zeitung</u>, and A B. Parsons, an Anarchist with a negro wife. The speeches were rather mild in tone, but when Sam Fielden, another Anarchist leader, mounted the wagon from which the orators spoke, the crowd pressed nearer, knowing that something different was coming.

They were not disappointed. Fielden spoke for 20 minutes, growing wilder and more violent as he proceeded. Police Inspector Bonfield had heard the early part of the speech, and, walking down the street to the Des Plaines-street police station, not 300 feet south of where Fielden stood, called out a reserve of 60 policemen and started them up the street toward the crowd. The men were formed in two lines stretching from curb to curb. The Inspector hurried on ahead, and, forcing his way through the crowd, reached a point close to the wagon. Fielden had just uttered an incendiary sentence, when Bonfield cried:

"I command you in the name of the law to desist, and you," turning to the crowd, "to disperse."

Just as he began to speak the stars on the broad breasts of the blue coats, as they came marching down the street so quietly that they had not been heard, reflected the rays of light from the neighboring street lamp. From a little group of men standing at the entrance to an alley opening on Des Plaines-street, opposite where Fielden was speaking, something rose up into the air, carrying with it a slender tail of fire, squarely in front of the advancing line of policemen. It struck and sputtered mildly for a moment. Then, as they were so close to it that the nearest man could have stepped upon the thing, it exploded with terrific effect.

The men in the centre of the line went down with shrieks and groans, dying together. Then from the Anarchists on every side, a deadly fire was poured in on the stricken lines of police, and more men fell to the ground. At the discharge of the bomb the bystanders on the sidewalk fled for their lives, and numbers were trampled upon in the mad haste of the crowd to get away. The groans of those hit could be heard above the rattle of the revolvers, as the police answered the fire of the rioters with deadly effect. In two minutes the ground was strewn with wounded men. Then the shots straggled, and soon after all was quiet and the police were masters of the situation.

The situation was appalling in the extreme. The ground was covered with the bodies of men writhing in agony and apparently dying. The men who were uninjured were ministering to their comrades as best they could, and as soon as possible the wounded were removed to the station house. The first death was that of Officer Joseph Deegan, who rose from the ground where he was thrown by the explosion, walked a hundred feet toward the station house, and, dropping down, expired. All around within a radius of a block of the field of battle men were seen limping into drug stores and saloons or crawling on their hands, their legs being disabled. Others tottered along the street like drunken men, holding their hands to their heads and calling for help to take them home. The open doorways and saloons in the immediate vicinity were crowded with men. Some jumped over tables and chairs, barricading themselves behind them; others crouched behind the walls, counters, doorways, and empty barrels. For a few minutes after the shooting nobody ventured out on the street.

A hospital was hastily improvised in the squad room at the station house, and thither the wounded were carried by tender hands. The room presented a harrowing sight. Half a dozen men, from whom the blood literally flowed in streams, were stretched upon the floor. Others were laid out on tables and benches, and others not so badly wounded were placed in chairs to await, with what patience they could, the assistance of the surgeon. Mattresses and other bedding were dragged down stairs and dozens of willing hands did their utmost to assuage the pain of the sufferers. Very soon the doctors were busy with needle, lancet, and probe. Priests passed from one wounded man to another administering brief words of consolation and hope and the sacrament of extreme unction to others. Officers and volunteer assistants went around with stimulants, or helped to bind up wounds, or held the patient down while the Surgeon was at work or carried come of the wounded to the other apartments, or in some other way did what could be done to help in easing pain or saving life. Pools of blood formed on the floor and was tramped about until almost every foot of space was red and slippery.

The groans of the dying men arose above the heavy shuffling of feet, and, to add to the agony, the cries of women, relatives of officers reported to have been wounded, could be heard from an outer room, beyond which the women were not permitted to enter. Men who had only got a foot or an arm wounded, even though the blood poured from it in streams, sat still, claiming no help in the face of the greater agony. "O Christ! Let me die!" "O merciful God!" and similar expressions were continually wrung forth as the surgeon's knife or saw was at work or when attempts were made to move those more badly wounded. The sacrament of extreme unction was administered to eight of the wounded before they were moved from the spot where they had been first laid.

As the bodies were picked up from the ground it was found that one man, an unknown Bohemian, was dead, making, with Officer Deegan, two victims already of the crime . . .

Lieut. Bowler, who was in charge of the Second Company of 24 men, said: "Every man in my company is wounded, with only three exceptions. I led the company up to the wagon from which the speeches were being made. Inspector Bonfield and Capt. Ward were immediately in front of me. The Inspector told Fielden they would have to stop, as he had orders to disperse the meeting. As he finished speaking a bomb was thrown from the wagon and fell directly in the centre of my company, where it exploded."

"Are you positive the bomb was thrown from that wagon?"

"Yes, I am. I could make no mistake about it, for I saw it thrown. Officers Reid and Doyle were knocked down by it. Bonfield, Ward, and myself were the only three to escape. Every one behind me was wounded -- just mowed down."

Several of the men listening to Felden had their revolvers in their hands under their coats, and were prepared for an attack. These drifted around to the northern end of the crowd, where the street was much darker. The windows of the brick building in the northeastern corner of Randolph and Desplaines streets were filled with the heads and faces of men and women. One of the wounded officers says he saw the bomb coming from one of these windows. Officer Marx said he saw the bomb coming from the wagon in which the speakers stood. It is probable that both of the officers were mistaken and that the bomb came from the sidewalk. . . .

THE CHICAGO SANITARY DISTRICT - 1889

In 1889, the Illinois State Legislature created the Chicago Sanitary District. It was designed to clean up the Chicago River and provide for the proper disposal of sewage. A portion of this act follows.

(Source: Laws of the State of Illinois, 36th General Assembly, 1889.)

SECTION 1. Be it enacted by the People of the State of Illinois, represented in the General Assembly: That whenever any area of contiguous territory within the limits of a single county shall contain two or more incorporated cities, towns or villages, and shall be so situated that the maintenance of a common outlet for the drainage thereof will conduce to the preservation of the public health, the same may be incorporated as a sanitary district under this act, in the manner following: Any 5,000 legal voters resident within the limits of such proposed sanitary district may petition the county judge of the county in which they reside, to cause the question to be submitted to the legal voters of such proposed district whether they will organize as a sanitary district under this act. Such petition shall be addressed to the county judge, and shall contain a definite description of the territory intended to be embraced in such district, and the name of such proposed sanitary district: Provided, however, that no territory shall be included in any municipal corporation formed hereunder which is not situated within the limits of a city, incorporated town or village, or within three miles thereof, and no territory shall be included within more than one sanitary district under this act. Upon the filing of such petition in the office of the county clerk of the county in which such territory is situated, it shall be the duty of the county judge to call to his assistance two judges of the circuit court, and such judges shall constitute a board of commissioners which shall have power and authority to consider the boundaries of any such proposed sanitary district, whether the same shall be described in such petition or otherwise. Notice shall be given by such county judge of the time and place where such commissioners will meet, by a publication inserted in one or more daily papers published in such county at least twenty days prior to such meeting. At such meeting, the county judge shall preside, and all persons in such proposed sanitary district shall have an opportunity to be heard touching the location and boundary of such proposed district and make suggestions regarding the same, and such commissioners, after hearing statements, evidence and suggestions, shall fix and determine the limits and boundaries of such proposed district, and for that purpose and to that extent, may alter and amend such petition. After such determination by said commissioners, or a majority of them, the county judge shall submit to the legal voters of the proposed sanitary district the question of the organization and establishment of the proposed sanitary district, as determined by said commissioners at an election to be held on the first Tuesday after the first Monday in November thence next ensuing, notice whereof shall be given by said commissioners, at least twenty days prior thereto, by publication in one or more daily papers published within such proposed sanitary district, such notice to specify briefly the purpose of such election, with a description of such proposed district. Each legal voter resident within such proposed sanitary district shall have the right to cast a ballot at such election, with the words thereon, "For Sanitary District," or, "Against Sanitary District." The ballots so cast shall be received, returned and canvassed in the same manner and by the same officers as is provided by law, in the case of ballots cast for county officers. The county judge shall cause a statement of the result of such election to be spread upon the records of the county court. If a majority of the votes cast upon the question of the incorporation of the proposed sanitary district shall be in favor of the proposed sanitary district, such proposed district shall thenceforth be deemed an organized sanitary district under this act.

2. All courts in this State shall take judicial notice of the existence of all sanitary districts organized under this act. Upon the organization of any sanitary district under this act, the county judge shall call an election to elect officers, and cause notice thereof to be posted or published, and perform all other acts in reference to such election in like manner as nearly as may be as he is required to perform in reference to the election of officers in newly organized cities under the provisions of an act entitled "An act to provide for the incorporation of cities and villages," approved April 10, 1872.

3. In each sanitary district organized under this act, there shall be elected nine trustees who shall hold their offices for five years, and until their successors are elected and qualified, except the term of office of the first trustees elected, shall be until five years after the first Monday in December after their election. The election of trustees, after the first, shall be on the Tuesday next after the first Monday in November, in every fifth year. In all elections for trustees, each qualified voter may vote for as many candidates as there are trustees to be elected, or he may distribute his vote among not less than five-ninths of the candidates to be elected, giving to teach of the candidates among whom he distributes the same, the same number of votes or fractional parts of votes. The trustees shall choose one of their number president, and such sanitary district shall, from the time of the first election held by it under this act, be construed in law and equity a body corporate and politic and by the name and style of the sanitary district . . . ., and by such name and style may sue and be sued, contract and be contracted with, acquire and hold real estate and personal property necessary for corporate purposes, and adopt a common seal and alter the same at pleasure . . .

THE WORLD'S COLUMBIAN EXPOSITION - 1890

In 1893, Chicago hosted a World's Fair, known as the World's Columbian Exposition. Three years earlier, President Benjamin Harrison issued a proclamation proclaiming Chicago the site of this giant exhibition. What follows is that official proclamation.

(Source: <u>Messages and Papers of the Presidents,</u> XII, New York, 1897.)

BY THE PRESIDENT OF THE UNITED STATES OF AMERICA.
A PROCLAMATION

Whereas satisfactory proof has been presented to me that provision has been made for adequate grounds and buildings for the uses of the World's Columbian Exposition, and that a sum not less than $10,000,000, to be used and expended for the purposes of said exposition, has been provided in accordance with the conditions and requirements of section 10 of an act entitled "An act to provide for celebrating the four hudredth anniversary of the discovery of America by Christopher Columbus, by holding an international exhibition of arts, industries, manufactures, and the products of the soil, mine, and sea, in the city of Chicago, in the State of Illinois," approved April 25, 1890:

Now, therefore, I, Benjamin Harrison, President of the United States, by virtue of the authority vested in me by said act, do hereby declare and proclaim that such international exhibition will be opened on the 1st day of May, in the year 1893, in the city of Chicago, in the State of Illinois, and will not be closed before the last Thursday in October of the same year. And in the name of the Government of the people of the United States I do hereby invite all the nations of the earth to take part in the commemoration of an event that is preeminent in human history and of lasting interest to mankind by appointing representatives thereto and sending such exhibits to the World's Columbian Exposition as will most fitly and fully illustrate their resources, their industries, and their progress in civilization.

In testimony whereof I have hereunto set my hand and caused the seal of the United States to be affixed.

[Seal.] Done at the city of Washington, this 24th day of December, 1890, and of the Independence of the United States the one hundred and fifteenth.

BENJ. HARRISON

By the President:
JAMES G. BLAINE, <u>Secretary of State.</u>

THE PULLMAN STRIKE - 1894

In the summer of 1894, one of the great labor disturbances in the history of the United States took place in Chicago. This was the Pullman Strike. What follows is the order given by President Grover Cleveland, over the protests of Illinois Governor John P. Altgeld, sending troops into the city to restore order. The second selection is a small excerpt from the official report of the Senate Commission appointed to investigate the strike.

(Source: James D. Richardson, ed., Messages and Papers of the Presidents, XIII, New York, 1897; U.S. Strike Commission, Report on the Chicago Strike, June-July, 1894, Senate Executive Doc. No. 7, 53rd Cong., 3rd Sess., XVIII-XIX.)

BY THE PRESIDENT OF THE UNITED STATES OF AMERICA
A PROCLAMATION

Whereas, by reason of unlawful obstructions, combinations, and assemblages of persons, it has become impracticable, in the judgment of the President, to enforce by the ordinary course of judicial proceedings the laws of the United States within the State of Illinois, and especially in the city of Chicago within said State; and

Whereas, for the purpose of enforcing the faithful execution of the laws of the United States and protecting its property and removing obstructions to the United States mails in the State and city aforesaid, the President has employed a part of the military forces of the United States:

Now, therefore, I, Grover Cleveland, President of the United States, do hereby admonish all good citizens and all persons who may be or may come within the city and State aforesaid against aiding, countenancing, encouraging, or taking any part in such unlawful obstructions, combinations, and assemblages; and I hereby warn all persons engaged in or in any way connected with such unlawful obstructions, combinations, and assemblages to disperse and retire peaceably to their respective abodes on or before 12 o'clock noon on the 9th day of July instant.

Those who disregard this warning and persist in taking part with a rioting mob in forcibly resisting and obstructing the execution of the laws of the United States or interfering with the functions of the Government or destroying or attempting to destroy the property belonging to the United States or under its protection can not be regarded otherwise than as public enemies.

Troops employed against such a riotous mob will act with all moderation and forbearance consistent with the accomplishment of the desired end, but the stern necessities that confront them will not with certainty permit discrimination between guilty participants and those who are mingled with them from curiosity and without criminal intent. The only safe course, therefore, for those not actually unlawfully participating is to abide at their homes, or at least not to be found in the neighborhood of riotous assemblages.

While there will be no hesitation or vacillation in the decisive treatment of the guilt, this warning is especially intended to protect and save the innocent.

In testimony whereof I have hereunto set my hand and caused the seal of the United States to be hereto affixed.

Done at the city of Washington, this 8th day of July, A.D. 1894, and of the Independence of the United States the one hundred and nineteenth.

[SEAL]

GROVER CLEVELAND

By the President:
 W.Q. GRESHAM,
  Secretary of State.

. . . According to the testimony of the railroads lost in property destroyed, hire of United States deputy marshals, and other incidental expenses, at least $685,308. The loss of earnings of these roads is estimated at $4,672,916. Some 3,100 employees at Pullman lost in wages, as estimated, at least $350,000. About 100,000 employees upon the 24 railroads centering at Chicago, all of which were more or less involved in the strike, lost in wages, as estimated, at least $1,389,143. Many of these employees are still adrift and losing wages.

Beyond theese amounts very great losses, widely distributed, were incidentally suffered throughout the country. The suspension of transportation at Chicago paralyzed a vast distributive center, and imposed many hardships and much loss upon the great number of people whose manufacturing and business operations, employment, travel, and necessary supplies depend upon and demand regular transporation service to, from, and through Chicago.

During the strike the fatalities, arrests, indictments, and dismissals of charges for strike offenses in Chicago and vicinty were as follows:

Number shot and fatally wounded	12
Number arrested by police	515
Number arrested under United States statutes and against whom indictments were found	71
Number arrested against whom indictments were not found	119

The arrests made by the police were for murder, arson, burglary . . . .

PROSTITUTION IN CHICAGO - 1894

Prostitution has always been a serious problem in urban America, and the situation in Chicago has been no exception. The following brief selection describes the vice and corruption that prevailed in the city.

(Source: William T. Stead, <u>If Christ Came to Chicago!</u>, London, 1894.)

The lost women, these poor sisters of Christ Jesus, the images in which we have fashioned a womanhood first made in the image of God, are as numerous in Chicago as in any other great city. The silent vice of capitals abounds here at least to the same extent that it prevails in other cities of the million class. Where there are a million inhabitants it is probably an under estimate if it is assumed that there must be at least a thousand women who make their living not intermittently but constantly by means of prostitution. These regulars of the army of vice constitute the solid core or nucleus of a host far more numerous of irregulars, who, either from love of license or from need of money, give way to a temptation which is always at hand. The inmates of the sporting houses, so called, are probably not one-tenth of the total number of women who regard their sex as legitimate merchandise.

Both sporting houses and 'roomers' may be found in all parts of the city, but there is no section in which they are so concentrated as in the district between Harrison and Polk, and between Clark and Dearborn Streets. It was there, in the centre of the heart of Chicago, that I found Maggie Darling in the house of Madame Hastings.

Madame Hastings is a familiar figure in the alsatis of more than one city. She is famous in Chicago courts as having been the defendant in the case which led to the practical ruling that the police could not arrest any one they pleased on a warrant made out against those mythical personages, Richard Roe or John Doe. Before she contested that case, strange though it may appear to those who are unfamiliar with the Turkish methods of Chicago 'justice,' a policeman armed with a warrant charging Richard Roe with an offence against the law could, on the strength of that document, arrest anybody at his own sovereign will and pleasure. Mary Hastings, being raided on such a warrant, appealed to the higher court, which, as was to be expected, promptly decided against the validity of the Richard Roe warrant and Mary's name became famous in a leading case . . .

THE CHICAGO STOCKYARDS - 1899

One of Chicago's most fascinating sights at the turn of the century were its famous stockyards, where cattle and hogs were brought by the tens of thousands to be slaughtered, or shipped out to waiting Eastern markets. The following selection is a description of the yards by Rudyard Kipling.

(Source: Rudyard Kipling, From Sea to Sea, London, 1899.)

. . . They say every Englishman goes to the Chicago stockyards. You shall find them about six miles from the city; and once having seen them will never forget the sight. As far as the eye can reach stretches a township of cattle-pens, cunningly divided into blocks so that the animals of any pen can be speedily driven out close to an inclined timber path which leads to an elevated covered way straddling high above the pens. These viaducts are two-storied. On the upper storey tramp the doomed cattle, stolidly for the most part, On the lower, with a scuffling of sharp hooves and multitudinous yells, run the pigs. The same end is appointed for each. Thus you will see the gangs of cattle waiting their turn -- as they wait sometimes for days; and they need not be distressed by the sight of their fellows running about in the fear of death. All they know is that a man on horseback causes their next-door neighbours to move by means of a whip. Certain bars and fences are unshipped, and, behold, that crowd have gone up the mouth of a sloping tunnel and return no more. It is different with the pigs. They shriek back the news of the exodus to their friends, and a hundred pens skirl responsive. It was to the pigs I first addressed myself. Selecting a viaduct which was full of them, as I could hear though I could not see, I marked a sombre building whereto it ran, and went there, not unalarmed by stray cattle who had managed to escape from their proper quarters. A pleasant smell of brine warned me of what was coming. I entered the factory and found it full of pork in barrels, and on another storey more pork unbarrelled, and in a huge room, the halves of swine for whose use great lumps of ice were being pitched in at the window. That room was the mortuary chamber where the pigs lie for a little while in state ere they begin their progress through such passages as kings may sometimes travel. Turning a corner and not noting an overhead arrangement of greased rail, wheel, and pulley, I ran into the arms of four eviscerated carcasses, all pure white and of a human aspect, being pushed by a man clad in vehement red. When I leaped aside, the floor was slippery under me. There was a flavour of farmyard in my nostrils and the shouting of a multitude in my ears . . .

THE TENEMENT HOUSE ORDINANCE - 1902

Like other American cities, Chicago had its slum sections and tenement house districts, and like other cities, was slow to take any effective regulatory action to control or improve these areas. What follows below is the first important tenement house ordinance enacted in the city.

(Source: Journal of the City Council of Chicago, Chicago, 1903.)

AN ORDINANCE

Regulating the construction, ventilation and sanitary requirements of all tenements and apartment buildings to be hereafter constructed.

Be it ordained by the City Council of the City of Chicago, as follows:

SECTION 1. As used in this ordinance:
(1) "Tenement House" is any house or building or portion thereof which is (a) intended or designed to be occupied or (b) leased for occupation, or (c) actually occupied, as a home or residence of three or more families living in separate apartments, each family doing cooking upon the premises; "New Tenement House" includes (a) every tenement house hereafter erected for which ground has not been broken (under a building permit heretofore issued) prior to the day of the taking effect of this ordinance, and includes every such new tenement house as shall be increased or diminished in size or as shall be otherwise altered after its erection, and (b) every building now or hereafter in existence not now used as a tenement house, but hereafter converted or altered to such use;
(2) "Apartment" is a room or suite of two or more rooms occupied or leased for occupation or intended or designed to be occupied as a family domicile;
(3) "Yard" is an open, unoccupied space on the same lot with a tenement house, separating every part of every building on the lot from the rear line of the lot:
(4) "Court" is an open, unoccupied space, other than a yard, on the same lot with a tenement house; a court not extending to a street, alley or yard is an inner court; a court extending to a street, alley or yard is an outer court, but every part of every such outer court which shall not be in a direct line of vision from the opening of such an outer court into a street, alley or yard shall, for the purposes of this ordinance, be deemed an inner court;
(5) "Shaft" includes exterior and interior shafts whether for air,

light, elevator, dumb waiter or any other purpose; a vent shaft is one used solely to ventilate or light a water closet compartment or bath room;

(6) "Public Hall" is a hall, corridor or passageway not within an apartment;

(7) "Stair Hall" includes the stairs, stair landings, and those portions of the public halls through which it is necessary to pass in getting from the entrance floor to the roof;

(8) "Basement" is a story partly, but not more than one-half -- "Cellar" is a story more than one-half -- below the level of the street curb nearest the building or below the level of the ground nearest the building, if such ground be higher than the level of such curb; a basement (but not a cellar) shall be counted as the first story of a tenement house; where the grade of a curb or of the ground adjacent to a tenement house varies, the mean or average grade of such curb opposite or ground upon the lot containing the tenement house shall be regarded as the grade of such curb or ground within the meaning of this ordinance;

(9) "Story" is that portion of a building between the top of any floor beams and the top of the floor beams next above;

(10) "Shall" is always mandatory and not directory and the mandate shall (positively or negatively, as the case may require) apply to and govern any alterations in any tenement house, or in any courts or yards connected therewith, and shall equally apply to and govern the conditions resulting from any such alterations, as well as the original conditions of such house, courts and yards, so long as the house remains a tenement house.

SEC. 2. Every new tenement house more than five (5) stories high shall be of fireproof construction (according to the definition of "fire-proof construction" contained in the Building Code of the City of Chicago); every new tenement house more than three (3) stories high, but not more than five (5) stories high shall be of slow-burning construction (according to the definition of "slow-burning construction" contained in the Building Code of the City of Chicago) with the cellar and basement construction including the floor construction of the first story above the cellar or basement, fireproof. The cellar and basement construction and the floor construction of the first story above the cellar or basement of every new tenement house three (3) stories or less in height shall be either slow-burning or fire-proof.

SEC. 3. Every non-fire-proof tenement house more than three (3) stories high shall be provided with a fire escape or fire escapes, such as are required by the Statutes of Illinois and the ordinances of Chicago, except that there shall be a metal stairway between the balconies of every such fire escape, securely fastened to the wall of the building, not less than two (2) feet six (6) inches wide with a proper hand-rail, instead of the usual vertical ladder; in every case each separate apartment shall have direct access to at least one such fire escape unless such apartment have access (without passing through any other apartment) to at least two (2) flights of stairs leading to the ground, one of which is outside of the building; every court in which there shall be a fire escape shall have direct and unobstructed access along the surface of the ground, without entering into or passing through or over any building, to a street, alley or yard.

SEC. 4. Every new fire escape shall be painted with two (2) coats of durable paint, one put on in the shop and the other at once upon the erection of such fire escape.

SEC. 5. Every tenement house shall have in the roof a bulkhead or scuttle, fire-proof or covered with fire-proof materials, with stairs leading thereto; but in existing tenement houses a ladder instead of stairs may be used in the top story. No such roof opening shall be less than two (2) feet by three (3) feet. No scuttle or bulkhead door, shall have upon it any lock, but may be fastened on the inside by movable bolts or hooks.

SEC. 6. Every new tenement house shall have at least two flights of stairs, which shall extend from the entrance floor to the roof. Such stairs and the public halls in every new tenement house shall each be at least three (3) feet wide in the clear and every apartment shall be directly accessible from an entrance hall by means of at least one such flight of stairs. If any existing tenement house be so altered as to increase the number of apartments therein by one-third or more, or if such building be increased in height so that the total height after such increase be more than four (4) stories, or if the stairs therein be damaged by fire or otherwise to an extent greater than one-half the value thereof, the entrance stair halls, entrance halls and other public halls of the whole building shall be made to conform to the requirements of this ordinance as to new tenement houses.

SEC. 7. In every tenement house all stairways shall be provided with proper banisters and railings.

SEC. 8. Every non-fire-proof new tenement house containing over sixty (60) rooms shall have one additional flight of stairs (over and above the flight hereinbefore provided for) for every additional sixty (60) rooms or fraction thereof; but if such house contains not more than ninety (90) rooms, in lieu of an additional stairway the stairs and public halls throughout the entire building may be at least one-half wider than is provided in Section 6 and 13 of this ordinance.

SEC. 9. Every fire-proof new tenement house containing over ninety (90) rooms shall have one additional flight of stairs (over and above the flights hereinbefore provided for) for every additional ninety (90) rooms or fraction thereof, but if such house contains not more than one hundred and thirty-five (135) rooms, in lieu of an additional stairway the stairs and public halls throughout the entire building may be made at least one-half wider than is provided in Section 6 and 13 of this ordinance.

SEC. 10. Every flight of stairs required in a tenement house shall have an entrance on the entrance floor from a street, alley or yard, or from a court which opens into a street, alley or yard. . . .

THE IROQUOIS THEATRE FIRE - 1903

Thirty-two years after the city's great fire, Chicago experienced a second major tragedy, when, in a matter of minutes, almost six-hundred people were burned to death in a fire that broke out in the Iroquois movie theatre. The following is a newspaper description of the holocaust.

(Source: New York Times, December 31, 1903.)

Between 550 and 600 lives were lost in ten minutes in a fire and panic in the new Iroquois Theatre between 3:15 and 3:25 yesterday afternoon. The Iroquois Theatre was the newest, the largest, and, as far as human power could make it, the safest theatre in Chicago.

It is on the north side of Randolph Street, between State Street and Dearborn Street. The stage backs up to Dearborn Street and faces east.

At the morgues are 566 bodies, 100 of which have been identified. More than 300 were injured and more than 200 are missing.

Of the dead, a few score were identified last night. Of the unidentified nearly all were so badly burned that recognition was impossible. Only by trinkets and burned scraps of wearing apparel will the bodies of scores be made known to their families.

All night long a horror chained, persistent throng of those whose friends and relatives were numbered among the missing lifted blanket after blanket in the search through the morgues of the city.

Not since the fire of 1871 has Chicago been visited by such a tragedy. It was over before the city knew that it happened: the news left paralysis behind.

Large Audience Present.

"Mr. Blue Beard" was being performed in the theatre. An audience not only of unusual size, but of unusual composition, was listening to it. It was the matinee audience of the mid-holiday season. Only once in a year could such an audience have gathered; only once in all the twelve months could so many children have been collected within the walls of the theatre. And on this one occasion the sacrifice to flame was demanded.

There were men in the audience, and in the galleries, from which the greatest tribute was demanded, but they were few in proportion to the children. Women died with their arms around their children. There were 2,000 persons or thereabouts in the theatre. Of that number 1,740 had seats.

The rest were massed in the rear of seats on the floor and the first balcony. In the galleries, even the rear seats of the seated gallery, were seated persons who ordinarily would have not been content with anything less than parquet seats. They were mothers, aunts, and elder sisters taking the children for an outing which fitted only to the one afternoon; young fellows from college treating their visiting chums to the theatre; schoolgirls out with their young friends for the same kind of a lark.

Such was the human material provided on one side of the curtain. On the other were 300 members of the extravaganza company. They were dressed in flimsy garments trailing with gauze, veils of death once the breath of fire swept over them. Between audience and performers was the curtain line, down which an asbestos fire curtain should have fallen one second after the alarm was given. The curtain never fell.

The fire leaped from the stage as if from a furnace door. The draught from the open stage exits behind drove it upward to the galleries. Over a carpet of the dead it forced its own way through the chimney of the alley doors on the galleries.

The newest theatre in Chicago, the playhouse declared to be fireproof from dressing room to capstone, burned till it was a steel skeleton and its wrecked interior a charnel house. The Coroner to-morrow will begin to learn who, if any one, was to blame; the Building Commissioner will endeavor to learn if the building was overcrowded, and if all the fire ordinances were obeyed.

Asbestos Curtain Did Not Fall.

The only thing plain last night was that the asbestos curtain did not fall. The flyman of the theatre, Charles Johnson, says that for some time past it had been the practice at the theatre to have the curtain high at night so as to permit a good view of the aerial ballet. "They attempted to drop the curtain," he said, "but it would not drop below the height it had been fixed at."

The report made to Manager Will J. Davis was that the curtain caught when a little way down and bulged out under the force of the terrific draught. "Men tried to pull it down," he said. "It would not come." Another report in circulation was that the assistant stage manager, who had immediate charge of the curtain, was not on the stage, but in the audience. He, it was declared, would have touched an electric button, which would have operated the sheet in a second. Without him, according to this rumor, the attempt was made clumsily to run the curtain down by hand.

The fire started while the double octette was singing "Pearly Moonlight." Eddie Foy, of the stage, was making up for his "elephant" specialty.

On the audience's left -- the stage right -- a line of fire flashed straight up. It was followed by a noise as of an explosion. According to early accounts, however, there was no real explosion, the sound being that of the fuse of the "spot" light.

This light caused the fire. On this all reports of the stage folk agree. As to the manner accounts differ widely. R.M. Cumminging, the boy in charge of the light, said last night that it was short circuited. Stage hands, as they fled from the scene, however, were heard to question one another, "Who kicked over the light?" The light belonged to the "Mr. Bluebeard" company.

The beginning of the disaster was slow. The stagehands had been fighting the line of wavering flame along the muslin fly border for some seconds before the audience knew anything was the matter. The fly border was tinder to the fire. Made of muslin, it was saturated with paint. The stagehands grasped the long sticks used in their work. "Hit it with the sticks!" was the cry. "Beat it out, beat it out!"

The men struck savagely. A few yards of the border fell upon the stage, and were stamped to charred fragments.

That sight was the first warning the audience had. For a second there was a hush. The players halted in their lines; the musicians ceased to play.

Then the murmur of fear ran through the audience. There were cries from a few, followed by the breaking, rumbling sound of the first step toward the flight of panic.

Eddie Foy's Coolness.

At that moment a strange figure appeared upon the stage. It wore tights, a loose upper garment, and the face was one-half made up. It was Eddie Foy, chief comedian of the company.

Before he reached the centre of the stage he had called out to a stage hand:

"Take my Bryan, there; get him out there by the stage way."

The stage hand grabbed the little chap. Foy saw him dart with him to safety as he turned his head.

Freed of parental anxiety, he faced the audience.

"Keep quiet!" he shouted; "quiet! Go out in order."

Between exclamations he bent over toward Herbert Dillea, the orchestra leader. "Start an overture," he commanded; "start anything. For God's sake, play and keep on playing."

The brave words were as bravely answered. Dillea raised his wand and the musicians began to play. Better than any one in the theatre they knew the peril. They could look up and see that the 300 sets of the "Mr. Blue Beard" scenery all were ablaze. Their faces were white, their hands trembled, but they played, and played.

The curtain started to come down. It stopped, it swayed as from a heavy wind, and then it "buckled" near the centre. From that moment no power short of omnipotent could have saved the occupants of the upper gallery.

The coolness of Foy, of Dillea, and of others players, who begged the audience to hold itself in check, however, probably saved many lives on the parquet floor. Panic prevailed, but the maddest of it, save in the doomed gallery, was at the outskirts of the ground floor crowd.

Those in greatest danger through proximity to the stage did not throw their weight against the mass ahead. Not many died on the first floor, proof of the contention that some restraint existed in this section of the audience.

Women were trod under foot near the rear. Most at this point, however, were rescued by the determined rush of the policemen at the entrance and of the doorkeeper and his assistants. The theatre had thirty exits. All were opened before the fire reached full headway, but some had to be forced open.

Only one door at the Randolph Street entrance was opened, the others being locked, according, it appears, to custom, from within and without; these doors were shattered in the first two minutes after the fire broke out.

Doors Difficult to Open.

The doors of the exits on the alley side, between Randolph and Lake Streets, in one or more instances are declared by those who escaped to have been either frozen or rusted. They opened to assaults, but priceless seconds were lost.

Before this time, Foy had run back across the stage and reached the alley. With him fled the members of the aerial ballet, the last of the performers to get out.

The aerialists owed their lives to the boy in charge of the fly elevator. They were aloft in readiness for their flight above the heads of the audience. The elevator boy ran his cage up even with the line of fire, took them in, and brought them safely down.

As Foy and the group reached the outer doorway the stage loft collapsed, and tons of fire poured over the stage. The lights went out in the theatre with this destruction of the switchboard and all stage connections. One column of flame rose and swished along the ceiling of the theatre. Then this awful illumination also was swallowed up. None may paint from personal understanding that which took place in that pit of darkness.

In spite of the terrible form of the destruction, it came swiftly enough to shorten pain. This, at least, was true of those who died in the second balcony, striving to reach the alley exits abreast of them. Six and seven feet deep they were found, not packed in layers, but jumbled and twisted in struggle with one another.

Opposite the westernmost exit of the balcony was a room in the Northwestern University Building, where painters were working, wiping out the traces of another fire.

They heard the sound of the detonation of the fuse and the rush of feet toward the exit across the way. Out on the iron stairway came a man, pushed by a power behind himself crazy with fear. He would have run down the iron fire-escape, but flame, bursting out of the exit beneath, wrapped itself around the iron ladder.

"A ladder!" shouted one of the painters. "Run it out." It was run out. The man started to cross. The ladder slipped on the frosty window casing. Its burden was precipitated down on the icy ground. The first of the arriving firemen picked up the broken form. . . .

THE CHICAGO PLAN COMMISSION - 1909

After considerable discussion, the City Council created the Chicago Plan Commission, whose purpose was to develop a comprehensive plan for the improvement and future development of the city. Charles H. Wacker was appointed chairman; and Daniel Burnham, chief consulting architect.

(Source: Chicago Plan Commission, Proceedings, Chicago, November 4, 1909.)

. . . The result of these efforts is now presented to you in the book called the "Plan of Chicago," which represents over three years of hard work on the part of the committee, during which time more than four hundred meetings were held. In this book, prepared under the direction of the Commercial Club, by Daniel H. Burnham and Edward H. Bennett, architects, and edited by Charles Moore, corresponding member of the American Institute of Architects, the genius of Daniel H. Burnham has pointed out the great possibilities for improving and beautifying our city.

In producing the "Plan of Chicago" the club engaged, without stint of money, the best talent that could be obtained, and, it should be added, the Commercial Club realizes that it could not have accomplished as much as it did had it not been for the co-operation of the press, Governor Deneen, Mayor Busse, the members of the legislature and the city council, the park boards and all public bodies and officials whose aid was required, and in addition thereto the liberal support given the club by public-spirited fellow-citizens.

This book was presented to the Mayor with a suggestion that the city council of the City of Chicago be requested to authorize the appointment of a commission, the purpose of which is fully, clearly and concisely set forth in the Mayor's message to the city council on July 6, 1909, as follows:

"I desire to bring to your attention, with a view to future action, the so-called Chicago Plan for the development and improvement of our city, with which plans you have all doubtless been made acquainted by newspaper publication and otherwise, and which has been, or soon will be, laid before you in detail.

"In my judgment, the men who have fathered this project have done a most important work for their city and their fellow-citizens. They have labored unselfishly as volunteers. They have given freely of their time and energy and money for a number of years to produce a clear, concrete and comprehensive plan of municipal development calculated to utilize the natural advantages of Chicago in the direction of making it a beautiful and attractive city as well as a commercial metropolis. I am now asked to present the result of their work to you with a view to securing your co-operation, and, in presenting it, to make clear certain points, as follows:

"1. The central idea out of which the Chicago Plan has grown, as I understand it, is this: If Chicago is to become, as we all believe, the greatest and most attractive city of this continent, its development and improvement should be guided along certain definite and pre-arranged lines, to the end that the necessary expenditures for public improvements from year to year may serve not only the purpose of the moment, but also the needs of the future; and from time to time and piecemeal, as necessity calls for them, may in the long run fit into and become parts of a well-considered, consistent, practical, organized scheme of municipal development.

"2. The Chicago Plan has been formulated as a basis and starting point, as it were, from which to work in the development of an official municipal plan that shall embrace the making of public improvements and the development of public utilities in coming years. It is not presented to us as a hard and fast plan to be accepted or rejected as it stands. It is presented more as a suggestion of the possibilities of our situation, to be utilized in whole or in part in the development of an official plan, as the best judgment of this community may determine.

"3. The Chicago Plan is not presented as a scheme for spending untold millions of dollars now or in the future; on the contrary, it is a comprehensive suggestion of what may be accomplished in the course of years, it may be fifty, it may be a hundred, by spending, in conformity with a well-defined plan, the money which we must spend anyhow from time to time on permanent public improvements. Paris had been made the world's most beautiful city because she has followed for more than fifty years the policy of making public improvements in conformity with a clearly defined plan. If the Chicago plan were adopted now, a good start towards its realization could be made at once and without a dollar of cost to the people by having the refuse and excavated materials, disposition of which is becoming a burden, dumped in the lake at specified localities for the making of islands, outer parks, etc.

"4. The Chicago Plan is in conflict with no other plan or project for the industrial or commercial development of Chicago. It fits in with the recommendation of the Harbor Commission; it takes into account and provides for the city's growing transportation needs, both in relation to steam roads and in relation to transportation within the city limits, and communications between the different divisions of the city.

"5. . . . the men who have produced the Chicago Plan are all hard-headed business men whose interests individually and collectively are bound up absolutely with the industrial and commercial growth of this city. They are men who have learned by experience and observation that development and beautification, if you please, making Chicago attractive to visitors from all parts of the world, will add to Chicago's resources a very great commercial asset, the value of which will be reflected in every piece of real estate within our limits. In producing this plan they have particularly had in mind relief from the neglect from which the great West Side has suffered and for the congestion at the city's commercial center, which has so impeded healthy growth of the entire business. . . .

THE EASTLAND TRAGEDY - 1915

On July 24, 1915, the excursion steamer Eastland turned over at her pier in the Chicago River with a loss of 1,800 lives. It was the city's third great tragedy. The following selections are a description of the catastrophe, and an eyewitness account.

(Source: New York Times, July 25, 1916.)

Chicago, July 24. -- Approximately 1,800 persons, most of them women, children and babies, lost their lives in the murky little stream called by courtesy the Chicago River, this morning, when the excursion steamer Eastland turned over at her pier between Lasalle and Clark Streets.

There were 2,500 passengers on the Eastland and a crew of 72, commanded by Captain Henry Pedersen, according to a statement issued this evening by W.J. Greenbaum, general manager of the Indiana Transportation Company, after he had checked up the returns of the ticket takers.

At midnight 880 bodies had been taken to morgues and the work of taking out the bodies was still proceeding.

Beside these, 762 persons are known to have been rescued, and careful checking has shown 921 missing. It is feared that practically all the missing are drowned. This would make the death list about 1,800.

Trying to Fix the Blame.

The task of establishing the causes and of fixing responsibility has begun. A special Federal Grand Jury, called by Judge Landis, will begin an investigation at once. State's Attorney Maclay Hoyne opened an inquiry within two hours after the tragedy.

Aboard the Eastland at the hour set for sailing, 7:40 A.M., were approximately 2,500 excurionists. Some say there were more and that the disaster was caused by overloading the steamer. It is known that United States Custom House officials boarded the boat a short time before she went down and caused between 400 and 500 persons to be removed on finding that the steamer was carrying many more passengers than allowed by law.

The excurionists were a part of those going to the annual picnic of the Western Electric Company to its employes. About 7,000 tickets had been distributed and a fleet of five steamers had been chartered to take the picnickers across the lake to Michigan City, Ind., where there was to be a big parade and great festivities. The Eastland was the first of the fleet scheduled to depart for Michigan City, and a great throng clamored for admittance.

Cables Never Cast Off.

The passengers aboard swarmed to the left side of the ship as the other steamers drew up the river toward the wharf. A tug was hitched to the Eastland, ropes were ordered cast off, and the steamer's engines started, but the Eastland did not budge. Instead, the ship began to list slowly but steadily toward its left side. Children clutched the skirts of mothers and sisters to keep from falling. The whole cargo was impelled toward the falling side of the ship and water began to enter the lower port holes.

None of the hawsers had been cast off. Orders had been given to cast off, notwithstanding that for a considerable time the boat had been gradually listing. Whe the order to cast off was given it was too late. Before it could be carried out the boat had turned on her side, the hawsers, still attached to the ship, tearing the piling from the pier. The hawsers are still attached to the semi-sunken steamer, the Federal and local authorities having given strict orders that they are not to be distrubed, pending investigation.

Screams from passengers attracted the attention of fellow-excursionists on the pier awaiting the next steamer. Wharfmen and picnickers soon lined the edge of the embankment, reaching out helplessly toward the wavering steamer.

For nearly five minutes the ship listed before it finally dived under. Then there was a plunge, with a sigh of air escaping from the hold, mingled with crying of children and shrieks of women, and the ship was on the bottom of the river.

All Over in Six Minutes.

Hundreds on the upper deck were thrown into the water, and a few escaped. Most of the other passengers caught below in the cabins or on the lower decks, perished without a chance for life. They were swallowed up in the sight of other thousands crowding the Clark Street Bridge, the wharves, and adjoining streets on their way to the other boats chartered for the excursion.

It was all a matter of only a few minutes. Many witnesses say it was all over in six minutes.

The surface of the river was thick with struggling people. Babies perished in sight of those on the docks and bridges. Men and women in a frenzied battle for life churned the water, then sank.

On the side of the boat were some who had clambered over the rail as the boat settled on its side. Some escaped without even wetting their feet. The whistles of tugs and excursion boats shrieked the alarm and boats put off. South Water Street commission men tossed barrels and crates and chicken boxes into the river, where they were seized by the drowning. Forty miles away at Lockport the Bear Trap Dam in the Drainage Canal was closed to stop the river's current. Fireboats and tugs spread out like a fan around the death ship and began the work of taking out the bodies.

One mother grasped her two children in her arms as she slipped from the steamer into the water. One child was torn from her, but she and the other were saved. Fathers were drowned after aiding their wives and children to safety.

Warehouses Become Morgues

Nearby streets and warehouses were turned into morgues. Bodies were piled in rows. Ambulances, vans, and delivery trucks were pressed into service as death wagons, while as fast as the bodies were taken out hundreds of physicians strove to bring back life.

At the south approach to the Clark Street Bridge respiration machines were operated on the sidewalk. Victims were worked over the moment they reached shore and emergency hospitals were established within a few feet of the wreck.

The Theodore Roosevelt, one of the five boats chartered for the excursion, which was moored on the opposite side of the Clark Street Bridge, was turned into a morgue and hospital.

As soon as the news became known, doctors and nurses by the hundreds volunteered and for hours strove in the work of resuscitation. Few were revived, however, for the bodies had been in the water too long. The spectacles were harrowing. Policemen wept as the bodies of women were taken out, with their babies still clutched to their bosoms in the grasp of death.

Chicago tonight sits in sackcloth and ashes, still counting its dead. The mortuary lists are still growing. Despair had settled over the city akin to that following the Iroquois Theatre fire. The Eastland calamity surpasses even the Iroquois disaster. Its roster of victims is greater. It is the worst excursion boat accident on record in America. It claimed more victims than the fire-scourged General Slocum on June 15, 1904, in New York Harbor, when 650 lives were lost.

Chicago Overwhelmed.

Business and social life have been at a standstill all day. The city is overwhelmed by the great disaster. Flags are at half staff on all buildings: there are crowds in the vicinity of the Chicago River which the police find difficult to hold in check, the downtown streets are congested with hearses and auto trucks carrying away the dead, and at the morgues there are lines of people stretching for blocks awaiting admission to identify and recover lost friends or relatives. In the horrors of the day strong men have wept like children, and some have become insane. Chicago never before suffered such a tragedy, and is overwhelmed with grief.

All day long and tonight great crowds thronged the river's edge and choked the streets leading to it. On the side of the boat which protruded several feet above the water groups of men gathered around holes burned with gas flames through the steel hull and with ropes dragged up the bodies as fast as the divers could get them. Many are still in the boat, while the river still holds bodies, and it will be days before the exact number of dead is established. . . .

THE CHICAGO RACE RIOT - 1919

In July, 1919, a savage race riot broke out in Chicago. It shocked Chicagoans and the nation at large. The following is an excerpt from the New York Times description of the event.

(Source: New York Times, July 28, 1919.)

Two negroes were killed and about fifty were injured, several probably fatally, when race rioting started at South Side beaches here this afternoon and spread into the heart of the Black Belt. Among the known wounded were two policemen and three women.

So great was the confusion throughout the district that the acting Chief of Police, Alcock, was unable late tonight to estimate the total number of injured. Scores received cuts and bruises from flying stones and rocks but went to their own homes for medical attention.

An incomplete list of the wounded follows:

Gallagher, Policeman Thomas, white, hit in head with brick.
Carroll, Arthur, white, cut over eye and about head.
Long, William, white, cut in head and back.
Wilkes, Mrs. Gladys, white, ankle cut and body bruised.
O'Brien, Policeman John F., white, shot in left arm.
Crawford, James, colored, shot in liver; may die.
Cormer, Charles L., white, shot in head; may die.

Cormer was sitting in the window of his home watching the rioting. He was hit by a negro sniper. He fell back into the front room, where a woman was seen to carry him to a davenport.

Although ill-feeling between whites and blacks on the South Side has extended over a period of months, emphasized by bomb explosions, some shooting, and numerous fights, today's riots seem to have had their start in petty quarreling at the beach.

Reports that negroes wandered across the dividing line to the white section of the beach and that whites amused themselves by throwing small stones at negro bathers appeared the most plausible cause. Soon after the fighting started, a negro fled pursued by several whites.

He took shelter behind a building and began shooting at a policeman who had joined the pursuit and who returned the fire. The negro finally surrendered.

Negro Fatally Wounded.

During the fight one negro was probably fatally wounded.

Twenty-ninth Street was soon packed with whites and blacks, the latter predominating. More fighting took place, and a few shots were fired as some of the negroes fled. Patrol wagons loaded with policemen raced to the scene.

A fire broke out in a small building and fire apparatus was blocked by the throngs. Negroes are said to have tried to drag the firemen from their seats.

During the fighting, rocks, bricks, and other missiles were hurled, both at the beach and at various points along Twenty-ninth Street and along State Street. White men were frequently attacked and beaten on State Street, the police said.

At the beach, while missiles were flying, a negro on a raft was reported to have been struck with a rock and hurled into the lake. Later the body of a negro was taken from the water.

A white man, a swimmer, also was reported hit and drowned.

With the police stations emptied of reserves and scores of others rushed from north and west side stations, Acting Chief of Police Alcock ordered every available policeman on duty to prevent further outbreaks. The small army of policemen succeeded in bringing about a fair semblance of order.

Blacks and whites swarmed through the South Side black belt and rioting spread throughout much of the district. Police reserves and detectives from all stations in the city were rushed to the scene. Special calls to the stations and hospitals for ambulances were sent by Chief Alcock.

Policeman Shot in Arm.

John O'Brien, a policeman attached to the Cottage Grove station, was attacked by a mob of negroes at Twenty-ninth and State Streets. Several shots were fired at him and he was injured in the arm. He drew his revolver on the surging mass and fired several times into the crowd. The crowd scattered, leaving three blacks moaning on the pavement.

One died before he could be taken to a hospital. The others, who were not identified, were rushed to the Hahnemann Hospital, but not until after negroes had made valiant attempts to recover the wounded. Several whites who are said to have participated in the rioting told policemen that they had seen two black bathers drown.

Racial feeling which had been on a par with the weather during the day, reached a climax soon after 5 o'clock when white bathers attempted to drive negroes out of the water at the foot of Twenty-ninth Street. A rock hurled at a white boy by a colored man on the beach added to the ill feeling. Then a free-for-all fight ensued.

Stones and rocks were tossed, and whites and blacks clashed in open combats. Even white and colored women got into the mixup. The screams and shouts of the rioters were heard as far south as Thirty-fifth Street and soon bathers and spectators, white and black, swarmed in from all sides.

Several took their fisticuffs into the lake and battled, while those on shore tossed stones. It was during this struggle that several are reported to have been drowned. . . .

A ZONING ORDINANCE - 1923

A major revision of the city's zoning was enacted by the city council in 1923. Among its new provisions was a clause which limited building at the street line to a height of 265 feet. A section of this ordinance follows.

(Source: Chicago Zoning Ordinance, April 5, 1923.)

AN ORDINANCE

Establishing a plan for dividing the City of Chicago into districts for the purpose of regulating the location of trades and industries and of buildings and structures designed for dwellings, apartment houses, trades, industries, and other specified uses, for regulating height, volume, and size of buildings and structures, and intensity of use of lot areas for determining building lines, and for creating a board of appeals.

Be it ordained by the City Council of the City of Chicago:

Section 1. Interpretation; Purpose. In interpreting and applying the provisions of this ordinance, such provisions shall in every instance be held to be the minimum requirements adopted for the promotion of the public health, safety, comfort, morals or welfare.

Section 2. Definitions. Certain words in this ordinance are defined for the purposes thereof (unless there is express provision excluding such construction or the subject matter or context is repugnant thereto) as follows:

(a) Words used in the present tense include the future; the singular number includes the plural and the plural the singular; the word "building" includes the word "structure."

(b) Alley -- A narrow thoroughfare upon which abut generally the rear of premises, or upon which service entrances of buildings abut, and is not generally used as a thoroughfare by both pedestrians and vehicles, or which is not used for general traffic circulation, or which is not in excess of 30 feet wide at its intersection with a street.

(c) Apartment House -- A building which is used or intended to be used as a home or residence for two or more families living in separate apartments.

(d) Auxiliary Use -- A use customarily incidental to and accessory to the principal use of a building or premises located on the same premises with such principal use.

(e) Block -- A block shall be deemed to be that property abutting on a street on one side of such street and lying between the two nearest intersecting or intercepting streets, or nearest intersecting or intercepting streets, or nearest intersecting or intercepting street and railroad right of way or waterway.

(f) Building -- A building is a structure entirely separated from any other structure by space or by walls in which there are no communicating doors or windows or similar openings.

(g) _Depth of Lot_ -- The depth of a lot is the mean distance from the front street line of the lot to its rear line measured in the general direction of the side lines of the lot.

(h) _Dwelling House_ -- A building used or intended to be used as a home or residence in which all living rooms are accessible to each other from within the building and in which such living rooms are accessible without using an entrance vestibule, stairway or hallway that is designed as a common entrance vestibule, or common stairway or common hallway for more than one family, and in which the use and management of all sleeping quarters, all appliances for cooking ventilating, heating, or lighting, other than a public or community service, are under one control.

(i) _Family_ -- One or more individuals living, sleeping, cooking, and eating on the premises as a single housekeeping unit.

(j) _Grade_ -- The finished grade of premises improved by a building is the elevation of the surface of the ground adjoining the building. The established grade of premises whether vacant or improved is the elevation of the sidewalk at the property line as fixed by the City. Where the finished grade is below the level of the established grade, the established grade shall be used for all purposes of this ordinance.

(k) _Garage_ -- A public garage, except as otherwise provided by this paragraph, is a building or premises arranged, designed, and intended to be used for the storage of motor vehicles for hire or reward, or which does not come within the definition of a private or community garage as herein set forth. A private garage is a building with ground area not in excess of 800 square feet arranged, designed, and intended to be used for the storage on the ground floor of not more than 4 individually owned passenger automobiles devoted to the private use of the owner, when such garage is located on the same premises, as an auxiliary use, with the residence or apartment or business of the owner of such automobiles so stored, and where no fuel is sold. A use as a private stable shall be subject to the same ground area regulations for the purposes of this ordinance as the regulations controlling the ground area of a private garage. Where two or more separate private garages, each having a ground area not in excess of 200 square feet, are located on the rear half of the premises, not more than one of such garages having a vehicle entrance on a public street, such garages collectively shall be deemed a community garage, but a group of two or more private garages on a single lot not so located or arranged or any one of which is in excess of 200 square feet in area shall be deemed a public garage.

(l) _Height of Building_ -- The height of a building shall be the vertical distance measured in the case of flat roofs from the mean level of the established grade to the level of the highest point of the under side of the ceiling beams adjacent to the street, and in the case of a pitched roof from such grade to the mean height level of the under side of the rafters of the gable. Where a block has a frontage on a two-level street the upper street level may be used to determine the height of building for a distance back from such frontage not in excess of one-half the depth of the block at right angles to such frontage, but not farther back than the alley most nearly parallel to such street in any case. Where a structure is set back from the street line, the mean level of the finished grade of the premises along the line of that part of the structure nearest the street line may be substituted for the established grade for the purpose of determining the height of a building. Where no roof beams exist or there are structures wholly or partly above the roof, the height shall be measured from the established grade or finished grade to the level of the highest point of the building.

(m) <u>Lot</u> -- A parcel of land or premises occupied, or which it is contemplated shall be occupied, by one building with its usual auxiliary buildings or uses customarily incident to it, including such open spaces as are required by this ordinance and such open spaces as are arranged and designed to be used in connection with such building, shall be deemed a lot for the purposes of this ordinance. A corner lot shall be deemed to be that property which has an area not in excess of 8,000 square feet, and which abuts on two streets making an angle on the lot side of not greater than 120 degrees.

(n) <u>Non-conforming Use</u> -- A non-conforming use is a use which does not comply with the regulations of the use district in which it is situated.

(o) <u>Public Space</u> -- A park, public square, or submerged land under the jurisdiction of a park district shall be deemed a public space.

(p) <u>Street</u> -- A thoroughfare used for public foot and vehicle traffic other than an alley as herein defined, shall be deemed a street.

(q) <u>Street Line</u> -- The street line is the dividing line between a street and the lot. The front street line shall be deemed to be the shortest street line.

(r) <u>Street Wall</u> -- The street wall, for the purposes of this ordinance, shall be deemed that wall or part of a wall of a building, or that part of the wall of a porch or other structure, nearest to and most nearly parallel with the street, extending more than 4 feet 6 inches above the finished grade.

(s) <u>Volume of Building</u> -- The volume of a building shall be the contents in cubic feet of that space between the grade used in determining the height of buildings and the mean level of the roof (except as otherwise specifically provided by Section 16, Paragraph (a),) including scenery lofts and other storage spaces, cooling towers, elevator bulkheads, towers, penthouses, water tanks or water towers, dormers, bays, covered ways, covered porches or other spaces not open to the sky, and courts, provided that certain courts or certain parts thereof opening on thoroughfares or public spaces, cornices projecting beyond the exterior walls, piers or columns, or the space under the projection of a cornice, chimneys, parapet walls, structures extending into thoroughfares . . . .

THE ST. VALENTINE'S DAY MASSACRE - 1929

On St. Valentine's Day, 1929, one of the most notorious mass murders in Chicago gangland history took place, when crime boss Al Capone ordered the execution of seven members of a rival mob. The following selection is a newspaper account of this celebrated crime.

(Source: New York Times, February 15, 1929.)

CHICAGO. Feb. 14. - Chicago gangland leaders observed Valentine's Day with machine guns and a stream of bullets and as a result seven members of the George (Bugs) Moran-Dean O'Banion, North Side gang are dead in the most cold-blooded gang massacre in the history of this city's underworld.

The seven gang warriors were trapped in a beer-distributers' rendezvous at 2,122 North Clark Street, lined up against the wall by four men, two of whom were in police uniforms, and executed with the precision of a firing squad.

The killings have stunned the citizenry of Chicago as well as the Police Department, and while tonight there was no solution, the one outstanding cause was illicit liquor traffic.

The dead, the greatest in point of numbers since Chicago gang killing began in 1924 with the assassination of Dean O'Banion, were the remnants of the "mob" organized by O'Banion, later captained by Hymie Weiss and Peter Gusenberg and recently commanded by George (Bugs) Moran.

Capone's Name Is Mentioned.

One name loomed in the police investigation under way this afternoon and tonight. It was that of Alphonse (Scarface) Capone, gang leader extraordinary.

Six of the slain gangsters died in their tracks on the floor of the North Clark Street garage, a block from Lincoln Park and its fine residential neighborhood. A seventh, with twenty or more bullets in his body, died within an hour.

The police found more than 100 empty machine gun shells strewing the floor of the execution room, and there was a report that Moran had been taken out alive by the marauders.

Police Commissioner William F. Russell and his First Deputy Commissioner, John Stege, were bewildered tonight over the fact that the ambush was arranged by two men in police uniforms, wearing police badges, and the fact that the other killers arrived at the scene in an automobile resembling a detective bureau squad car. . . .

Tonight an underworld round-up unparalleled in the annals of the Police Department is under way.

"It's a war to the finish." Commissioner Russell said. "I've never known of a challenge like this -- the killers posing as policemen -- but now the challenge has been made, it's accepted. We're going to make this the knell of gangdom in Chicago."

Reconstructing the massacre as it occurred, police and prosecuting officials were of the opinion that the men were victims of their own cupidity as well as the wrath of their enemies, for they had been stood up against the brick wall of the garage, their backs, rather than their faces. . . .

The machine-gunners probably sprayed the heap of dead on the floor and then the four executioners marched out.

A tailor glanced up from his pressing iron next door, and a woman living near by ran to the street. They saw what appeared to be two men under arrest, their hands in the air, followed by two policemen. The four climbed into what looked like a police squad car, a fifth man sitting at the wheel, the motor humming. The car roared south in Clark Street, sweeping around the wrong side of a street car, and was lost in the traffic.

When police arrived upon the scene they found six of the men dead. The seventh, Frank Gusenberg, was crawling on the floor toward Police Lieutenant Tom Loftus. Gusenberg died within an hour at the Alexandrian Hospital.

The majority of the victims were dangerous men, with reputations equal to the worst, Deputy Commissioner Stege said.

"Where is 'Bugs' Moran?" Stege asked when his officers discovered the automobile which Moran was supposed to own.

Then came the story that perhaps he was one of the men who walked out of the garage hands high above his head, followed by the pseudo policemen.

Squads were dispatched to seek Moran. Others were sent after information concerning "Scarface Al" Capone's whereabouts. The latter group came back with word that Capone was at his Winter home in Miami, Fla.

The police recalled that the Aiello brothers' gang of North Side Sicilians had a year or so ago affiliated themselves with the Moran gang, and that the Aiellos and the Caponites were deadly enemies. But no Aiellos were found.

Coroner Herman N. Bundesen reached the garage within a half hour after the fusillade. The bodies were photographed and searched. . . .

Lieutenants John L. Sullivan and Otto Erianson of the Homicide Bureau checked the identifications and kept records of search results.

Peter Gusenberg had a large diamond ring and $447 in cash.

Albert Weinshank proved to be the cousin of a former State representative of the same family name. Weinshank, who recently took an "executive position" with the Central Cleaners and Dyers Company, had only $18 in cash, but he had a fine diamond ring and a bankbook showing an account in the name of A.H. Shanks.

Then a body was identified as that of John Snyder, alias Adam Meyers, alias Adam Hyers, alias Hayes. It was said that Snyder was owner of the Fairview Kennels, a dog track rivaling Capone's Hawthorne course. Chief Egan was told that Snyder was the "brains" of the Moran "mob." Snyder had $1,399.

The body of Mays, the overall-clad mechanic, had only a few dollars in the pockets. He was the father of seven children. A machine gun bullet had penetrated two medals of St. Christopher.

The fifth of the five bodies in the row, flat on their backs with their heads to the south, was recorded as that of Reinhardt H. Schwimmer, an optometrist. Despite his having no police record, it is said that he recently boasted that he was in the alcohol business and could have any one "taken for a ride."

Closer to the door, face down, with his head to the east, lay John Clark, brother-in-law of Moran, and rated as a killer with many notches in his guns. His clothes contained $681.

Woman's Story Aids Police.

"Bullet marks on the wall," Captain Thomas Condon observed and it was seen that few of the pellets missed their marks, for there were only seven or eight places where the detectives were sure bullets had struck.

Each of the victims had six to ten bullets shot through him. A high-powered electric bulb overhead flooded the execution chamber with a glare of white light. Chained in a corner was a huge police dog, which strained on its fastenings and snarled at the detectives.

The police expressed amazement that the seven gangsters had been induced to face the wall and certain death without a struggle and without resistance.

"That bunch always went well armed," a police captain said.

An explanation was seen in the story of Mrs. Alphonsine Morin, who lives just across the street from the garage. She told of seeing men she thought were policemen coming out after hearing the shooting.

"Two men in uniforms had rifles or shotguns as they came out the door," she said, "and there were two or three men walking ahead of them with their hands up in the air. It looked as though the police were making an arrest and they all got into an automobile and drove away."

"Quite simple," Chief Egan commented. "They would never have got that gang to line up unless they came in police uniforms."

Typical of his life, Frank Gusenberg refused during his last hour to tell the police anything. He was conscious, but he kept defying the police who sought names from him.

Assistant State's Attorney David Stansbury was put in charge of the investigation tonight by State's Attorney John A. Swanson. The police, prosecutor and the Federal authorities were all working together to get trace of the slayers.

Theories about who plotted and carried out the execution were numerous. . . .

A CZECH BECOMES MAYOR - 1931

In 1931, Anton J. Cermak was elected Mayor of Chicago. He was the first Eastern European to be elected to the chief magistrate's office in the city. In his inaugural address, an excerpt of which follows, he devoted a large portion of his speech to the desperate financial situation then prevailing in Chicago, primarily caused by the depression then sweeping the nation.

(Source: Chicago City Clerk, Inaugural Message of Hon. A.J. Cermak, Mayor, April 21, 1931.)

To the Honorable, the Members of the City Council of Chicago, Council Chamber, Chicago:

Gentlemen -- I deem it appropriate at this time to address you briefly on what I regard as comparatively the more serious conditions in our municipal affairs.

The matter which I rank first in importance is the present financial condition of the City of Chicago and its relation to the ever-increasing burden of taxation which is being loaded upon our citizens. In the last four years, the City's tax rate has increased from 92 1/2c per hundred to 137c per hundred. In figures, the City's expenditures (including those for school administration) have increased from $152,716,412.18 in 1927 to $171,261,262.71 in 1930. The general tax bills just mailed out for 1929 taxes are from 19 to 25 per cent higher than those of 1928. The progressive increase in the item of loss and cost in tax collections indicates a startling increase in forfeiture of property for nonpayment of taxes, and glaring instances of excessive taxation amounting practically to confiscation are unfortunately matters of common knowledge.

Directly, the City is without power either to change the existing tax laws or to more equitably distribute the tax burden. The first is a matter of legislation. The second depends upon the honest, intelligent and efficient administration of the legally constituted tax assessing and tax reviewing bodies.

The City, however, through the combined efforts of its Mayor, its Council, and its Administrative Department heads can contribute materially to a reduction of taxes. Of every dollar paid in taxes in Cook County 32.3c goes to the City of Chicago for general corporate purposes and 33.1c goes for the administration of its schools. Obviously, every dollar needlessly spent by the City adds to the tax burden, and every dollar properly saved by careful numicipal administration decreases the tax burden. With your help and the active assistance of our department heads, I propose to reduce the cost of our municipal government to the lowest possible minimum consistent with effective functioning of our vital municipal services.

In order that there may be no misunderstanding of the conditions existing at the time I assumed office, let me direct your attention to the present state of departmental appropriations. In several of the departments rendering essential service, the expenditures made against appropriations up to April 11th, exceed the proportion of the fund which it appears should have been spent between January 1 and April 11; in other words, the period from January 1 to April 11 constitutes approximately 29 percent of the annual appropriation has already been spent.

Despite this condition, I confidently believe that by the elimination of incompetence, waste and the unnecessary duplication of services and the application of modern methods in ordinary use in well-ordered private businesses, the City can not only function for the remainder of the year within its unexpended budget balances but that a very considerable salvage can be effected. I am fully aware that will be no easy task. I will need your help. I will insist upon the active and sustained co-operation of every department and bureau head. I shall ask and confidently expect to receive, the aid of disinterested civic-minded citizens whom I shall call upon to assist in this necessary reorganization of the City's business. To these ends I shall ask your concurrence in the appointment by me of a "Mayor's Advisory Commission" composed of disinterested, non-partisan citizens whose functions will include a thoroughgoing study of every department of the City Government with the definite object in view of making practical constructive recommendations designed to accomplish the following specific purposes:

1. To consolidate the existing 32 separate departments of the City into a smaller number of principal departments so as to bring about a more responsible and harmonious direction of the City's affairs, eliminate unnecessary employees and terminate the existing duplication and overlapping of municipal services.

2. To standardize, so far as possible, contracts and specifications for municipal work and supplies so as to invite a much wider competition than has heretofore existed in the letting of such contracts and thus obtain fairer prices for the City; to improve the City's central purchasing administration, by providing approved safeguards in the purchase, handling, delivery and accounting for supplies, materials and equipment, and to encourage by every proper means a feeling in the business community that the City of Chicago is entitled to the same consideration in its contracts and purchases as are large private businesses, and that the City of Chicago on its part will deal fairly and honestly with the business public in its purchases of supplies and the letting of contracts.

3. To co-operate with the Civil Service Commission which I will appoint. . . .

THE CHICAGO MUNICIPAL CODE - 1931

One of Mayor Cermak's first official acts was to improve the quality and operation of the municipal government. After several months work, a new Code for the City of Chicago was issued. With some revisions, the major provisions of this code still guide Chicago's municipal government.

(Source: <u>Revised Chicago Code of 1931</u>, Chicago City Council, June 25, 1931.)

THE MAYOR

Section
1. Powers and functions.
2. Bond.
3. Officers - appointment of.
4. Supervision of officers.
5. Secretary - duties.

Section
6. Signature of mayor.
7. Release of prisoners.
8. Flags and decorations.
9. Mayor authorized to contract for release of future claims.

1. Powers and functions.] The mayor of the city of Chicago, in addition to the duties, powers and functions vested in him by statute as the chief executive officer of the city and those specifically vested in him by the ordinances of the city, shall have authority to act, or to designate the officer who shall act, in the enforcement of any ordinance of the city in all cases where an ordinance fails to specify the officer who shall be charged with the duty of enforcement.

2. Bond.] The mayor, before entering upon the duties of his office, shall execute a bond to the city in the penal sum of ten thousand dollars, with such sureties as the city council shall approve, conditioned for the faithful performance of the duties of his office.

3. Officers -- appointment of.] The mayor shall appoint, by and with the advice and consent of the city council, all officers of the city whose appointment is not by the laws of this state or the ordinances of the city otherwise provided for; and whenever a vacancy shall occur in any office which by law he is empowered to fill, he shall, within thirty days after the occurrence of such vacancy, communicate to the city council the name of his appointee to such office.

4. Supervision of officers.] The mayor shall supervise the conduct of all the officers of the city, and, as to all who are exempt from the provisions of the civil service act, he shall examine the grounds of all reasonable complaints made against any of them, and cause their violations of duty and other offenses, if any, to be promptly punished.

5. Secretary -- duties.] The mayor may appoint a secretary, whose duty it shall be to preserve and keep in the mayor's office all books and papers which are usually filed, or are required by law to be filed, therein; to deliver to the city council and to the respective departments of the city all messages from the mayor in writing; to attend the mayor's office during the usual office hours, and to perform such other duties as may be required of him by the mayor.

6. Signature of mayor.] The mayor's signature shall appear on all licenses and permits granted by the authority of the city council except as otherwise provided by law or ordinance. In all cases where the ordinances of the city require that the signature of the mayor shall be attached to any license, permit, contract, local improvement bond, or other written instrument, and in all cases where said ordinances require the mayor's approval in writing or endorsement in writing, the mayor may, in his discretion, affix his signature or cause his signature to be affixed in such manner as may be authorized by law.

7. Release of prisoners.] The mayor shall have the power and authority to release and discharge, at his discretion, any person imprisoned for the violation of any city ordinance. In each and every case in which such release shall be so made by the mayor he shall cause a proper record thereof to be made and notice thereof to be sent to the city council, accompanying such notice with a statement setting out his reasons for such release.

8. Flags and decorations.] The mayor shall have power and authority to display flags or other decorations on, in, or about the city hall or other public building belonging to the city, on such occasions as he may deem proper.

On or before the tenth day of June, annually, the mayor shall issue a proclamation requesting the observance of the anniversary of the adoption of the flag of the United States by a general display of our national emblem on the fourteenth day of June, and requesting the observance of such anniversary in such other manner as may be deemed appropriate.

9. Mayor authorized to contract for release of future claims.] Whenever, in the judgment of the mayor, the interests of the city will be safeguarded and protected by the making of a release to the city against claims for future damages to private property arising out of or resulting from the carrying out of any ordinance or ordinances of the city providing for a local or general improvement or a public work, where such release can be obtained upon the payment by the city of a consideration of one dollar, the mayor is hereby authorized and empowered to enter into a contract of release on behalf of the city of Chicago with the owner or owners of such private property and to pay to such owner or owners the sum of one dollar as consideration for the release to the city of claims for future damages which may arise out of or result from the carrying out of any ordinances of the city . . . .

THE CHICAGO WORLD'S FAIR - 1933

The following selection describes the opening of the Second Chicago World's Fair. The fair celebrated the Chicago centennial, and was called "A Century of Progress." Although President Roosevelt was unable to attend, he sent a message to the people of Chicago, and the organizers of the fair.

(Source: New York Times, May 28, 1933.)

CHICAGO, May 27. --The portals of The Century of Progress Exposition, Chicago's second world's fair, were thrown open to the peoples of all nations this morning. There were happy crowds, miles of pageantry, roaring cannon and bombs which, bursting in a cloudless sky, released hundreds of American flags.

Four hours of ceremony reached their climax in Soldier Field, where Postmaster General Farley dedicated the $37,500,000 exposition and delivered a message from President Roosevelt. Other speakers were Governor Horner, Mayor Kelly and Rufus C. Dawes, president of the fair corporation.

President Roosevelt's message hailed the exposition as timely, not only because it marked a century of accomplishment, but because it "comes at a time when the world needs nothing so much as a better mutual understanding of the peoples of the earth."

A miraculous moment came at 9:15 o'clock Central daylight time, 10:15 New York daylight time, tonight when the subtle power of a beam of light, which started forty years ago from the star Arcturus, was caught up by astronomers and transmitted by them in augmented volume to delicate lighting mechanism in the tower of the exposition's Hall of Science.

Instantly upon that contact the grounds, pavilions and waterways of the fair were drenched with light. Thousands of awed beholders broke into cheers.

The jubilation blended into the harmony of the national anthem. Bands, bells, choruses and a symphony orchestra filled plazas, promenades and palaces with music.

Far-flung lights swayed over the multitude. Thunder of cannon, swish of rockets and dipping of flags proclaimed the event.

Four observatories, Yerkes, Illinois, Harvard and Allegheny at Pittsburgh, had telescopes focused on Arturus from which they were to "trap" the star's ray by photoelectric cells, amplify them and relay them to the master switch at the fair.

Dr. Edwin B. Frost, the blind director of Yerkes, who conceived the lighting plan, gave the signal on the platform where a bulletin board flashed responses from the observatories. The astronomers were aided by Westinghouse, General Electric and Western Union engineers in guiding the ray to its destination.

Professor Philip Fox, director of the Adler Planetarium, maintained contact with the observatories and announced their responses as they came on schedule.

Harvard found clouds obscuring the star and resorted to artificial light, but Yerkes, at Williams Bay, Wis., and Illinois, at Champaign, Ill., and Allegheny at Pittsburgh had perfect visibility and were able to transmit the stellar beams.

The spirit of this world's fair, which is in celebration of the one hundredth anniversary of Chicago's incorporation as a village, was expressed by Mr. Dawes. . . .

The Opening Ceremonies.

Thousands of visitors crowded Soldier Field at 9 o'clock this morning for the start of the colorful parade and pageantry. They were entertained by symphony music and bursting bombs, while the great parade in which 10,000 persons joined was forming at Chicago and Michigan Avenues. The crowd lining Michigan Avenue was estimated to number 350,000.

A salute of nations, in which forty national groups of sixteen, wearing their native costumes and following their national banners, followed the symphony concert. Two guns were fired with the appearance of each flag and the band played bits of each national anthem.

The national groups were seated on a platform facing the reviewing stand, presenting a medley of colors, with the reds, greens, blues and yellows of the Slavic races, the Latins and the Orientals. All stood at attention with the military detachments on the grounds, while the band played the national anthem, terminating the Pageant of Nations.

A twenty-one gun salute was begun, heralding the approach of Postmaster General Farley and the first division of the parade.

The Chicago Black Horse troop, 106th Cavalry, Illinois National Guard, the Guard of Honor, was one of the most spectacular features of the parade. Next came automobiles with the top-hatted members of the official party, Mr. Farley smiling and waving to applauding spectators. Mr. Dawes, Governor Horner and Mayor Kelly rode with Mr. Farley and then came Harry S. New, United States Commissioner to the fair; Daniel C. Roper, Secretary of Commerce, and the Illinois Senators, James Hamilton Lewis and William H. Dieterich.

Airplanes Roar Overhead.

While the civic dignitaries were taking their seats in the reviewing stand, fifty airplanes of the United States Army Air Service from Langley Field roared overhead. In two groups they swooped south, each seeming almost to skim the east and west towers of the Sky Ride.

After this a long division of military detachments paraded into the stadium, Major Gen. Frank Parker, commander of the Sixth Corps Area, United States Army, riding with his staff in an automobile. Rear Admiral Wat T. Cluverius of the Great Lakes Naval Station and his staff led the navy detachment, which included a company of marines and the Illinois Naval Reserve.

Then followed the queen of the esposition and her court on seven huge floats bearing fifty pretty young women. . . .

The queen sat in a throne, wearing a court robe flashing with rhinestones and trailing the royal purple. A diadem surmounted her blonde hair and she held the sceptre of her authority as the queen of grace and beauty in her right hand. She smiled and bowed as she passed the reviewing stand in response to the acclamations that greeted her.

The Veteran's Division followed, led by the Grand Army of the Republic. There were detachments of Spanish War Veterans, Veterans of Foreign Wars, Disabled Veterans of the World War, American Legion, Polish Legion of American War Veterans, Belgian American War Veterans, British and Colonial Veterans, French Veterans, Italian War Veterans' Association and Polish Army Veterans' Association, the last wearing the blue uniforms of their country. Then came the blue capped white uniforms of the nurses of the American Red Cross.

There followed costumed delegations of Syrians, Belgians, the English, Scotch and Welsh, Czechoslovakians, Danes, Finns, Germans, Hungarians, Italians, Lithuanians, Moroccans, Norwegians, Poles, Swedes, Ukrainians and Yugoslavians.

PRESIDENT'S MESSAGE TO THE FAIR

I have already expressed my regrets to President Dawes of the exposition at my inability to fulfill my engagement to open the Century of Progress celebration, which I am sure will be one of the historic gatherings, and which I hope will be the inauguration of a century of even greater progress--progress not only along material line; progress not only of my own country, but a world uplifting that will culminate in the greater happiness of mankind, and release all peoples from the outworn processes and policies that have brought about such a commercial and industrial depression as has plagued every country on the globe.

Certainly the human intelligence that has accomplished the industrial and cultural results displayed at your exposition need not fall short of devising methods that will insure against another perilous approach to collapse such as that from which we are now emerging.

The long and painful story of the progress of mankind to the development of what we term civilization is divided into chapters each of which marks the overcoming of a curse on humanity. Slavery, private wars, piracy, brigandage and well-nigh universal tyranny have in turn been conquered and done away with. Plagues which in past centuries decimated populations at frequent intervals have been studied and medicine has triumphed over most of them. Here and there appear, perhaps, sporadic vestiges of intolerance and cruel despotism, but what a change from the world conditions in which they were practically universal!

Yet all of these have in their time been deemed the inescapable crosses of mankind--beyond human power to ameliorate, much less cure. The advance of science and the evolution of humanity and charity made it known to us that whatever is the result of human agency is capable of correction by human intelligence. Who is there of so little faith as to believe that man is so limited that he will not find a remedy for the industrial ills that periodically make the world shiver with doubt and terror.

Every convention of the peoples of the world brings nearer the time of mutual helpfulness, so I welcome the celebration you are now beginning. It is timely not only because it marks a century of accomplishment, but it comes at a time when the world needs nothing so much as a better mutual understanding of the peoples of the earth.

I congratulate Chicago and its guests and wish the exposition unbounded success--success as a show but more success in helping to bring about a binding friendship among the nations of the earth.

CHICAGO TOMORROW - 1945

The Chicago Plan Commission has always been active in developing comprehensive plans for the rebuilding and expansion of the city. What follows is an interpretation of the preliminary comprehensive plan for Chicago prepared by the Chicago Plan Commission in a pamphlet entitled Chicago Tomorrow: 1945.

(Source: Chicago Plan Commission, Chicago Tomorrow: 1945, Chicago, 1945.)

Planning a city is like planning one's life, and good city planning recognizes the aspirations of the city's people. Just as with the individual, it is proper that long-term plans be prepared for the city so that practical conclusions regarding short-term plans can be reached. Most of the ills that beset our city today are attributable to the many expedient measures that have been taken in the past without reference to their long-term consequences. Adequate solutions must be evolved in a spirit of dispassionate realism and with confidence and determination. There must be courage to chart a course now that will assure the accomplishment of needed improvements. There is need for speedy elimination of conditions detrimental to urban living. A municipal atmosphere wherein every Chicagoan may profitably work and play must be created. These needs are a challenge to Chicago. The Comprehensive City Plan, when completed, will be an answer to that challenge.

The re-constitution of the Chicago Plan Commission in 1939 by the City Council as suggested by Mayor Edward J. Kelly, with the direction that a city plan be prepared, was in recognition of the acute physical, social, and economic problems that were and still are causes of deep concern to all thoughtful citizens. During the years that have intervened, these problems have become worse and new ones have appeared.

The preliminary Comprehensive City Plan, prepared by the Chicago Plan Commission, is for the use of city officials and every other citizen. It is a guide-plan that will be of aid in all constructive efforts directed toward the physical improvement of the city. It offers a basis for orderly growth and redevelopment. Within its framework there is opportunity for every reasonable enterprise. Property owners can proceed with capital improvements with a greater degree of security; tenants can be assured of a more attractive living environment; and public officials can proceed with increased confidence to provide the essential public works needed in the realization of the greater Chicago charted by the Plan.

The Plan is "preliminary" inasmuch as further analysis and refinement of many planning details are being continued by the Commission. It has been issued at this time in order that the progress toward a city plan may be displayed and that the proposals can become useful to the public in reaching conclusions on current problems. Studies will be made of such vitally important matters as the improvement of railway and other transportation services and terminal facilities in collaboration with other agencies engaged in those fields. Commercial and industrial land uses will be more closely examined in efforts to suggest better organization of space. Other important projects, such as the government center proposed for the Central Business District, are being studied.

The basic structure of the City Plan has formulated after thorough consideration of the social, economic, and legal aspects bearing on the future of Chicago. Thus the Plan is not merely a presentation of physical designs but is a reflection of the many other fundamental conclusion that the Plan Commission has drawn.

A truly effective city plan must be a living thing. It never becomes final or static because, in order to be expressive of public needs and desires, it must always be flexible and capable of adjustment. Such changes as become necessary from time to time must always be made in an orderly manner.

Within the framework formed by thoroughfares, lines of transportation, edges of industrial districts, and publicly-owned lands, there are 514 neighborhoods, within each of which people can live in greater quietude and safety and still have convenient access to all necessary services and places of employment. Typically, a neighborhood will accommodate 6,000 to 8,000 people. Near its middle will be an educational, recreational, and cultural center comprised of a grade school, a small quiet part, and a playground. It will serve all age-groups at appropriate hours during each day and evening. Fast and through-moving traffic will be carried on thoroughfares around, and not through the neighborhood.

In the Plan, groups of related neighborhoods become communities-59 in number-each a small city of from 50,000 to 80,000 residents. The community will contain a high school, a large park and athletic playfield, a major shopping center, and other services that may not be available within the neighborhood.

The comprehensive plan of a city is the well-considered correlation of those immediate and long-term needs, purposes, and desires of the people which have been found suitable, feasible, and capable of expression in physical terms, presented as a guide to assist private individuals and public officials in the achievement of beneficial objectives through co-ordinated action. In origin it must be realistic; in scope it must be broadly inclusive; in outline it must be bold and imaginative; in detail it must be flexible. Such a plan provides the basic framework for directing the development of the city and prescribes interpretations to facilitate its realization. Within that framework, complete freedom to function under the law is accorded to both public and private enterprise.

As a means of popularizing the dynamic concept under which the Comprehensive City Plan of Chicago is being developed, a symbol has been devised which portrays graphically the content and organization of the plan. It is conceived as a wheel made up of seven segments, each representing a fundamental phase of urban living. . . .

MAYOR DALEY OF CHICAGO - 1955

The most powerful political boss the city of Chicago has ever had, has been Richard J. Daley; he has been Chicago's Mayor since 1955. What follows is Mayor Daley's first inaugural address.

(Source: Journal of the City Council of Chicago, Chicago, 1955.)

Tonight I find it difficult to express to the people of Chicago my mingled feeling of challenge and confidence, of pride and humility.

I have lived all my life in a neighborhood of Chicago -- all that I am I owe to the influence of my family, our neighborhood and our city.

I have a deep pride in being part of the life of that neighborhood. I share in its problems and I know the needs of its people. Chicago is a city of neighborhoods and I resolve to be the mayor of all the neighborhoods -- of all people of Chicago.

The aldermen of the city council are men who have been chosen by their communities to represent them. Their mission must be the same as mine.

Tonight we start our job of carrying out the mandate given us by our fellow citizens. I know you are as eager as I am to accept the challenge of making our neighborhoods and our city a better place in which to live.

The structure of our city government follows the general pattern of American government in that it has legislative, executive and judicial branches.

The legislative branch is the city council, the executive -- the mayor.

This is a council governed city.

The aldermen were selected by the voters in their wards to represent their will. The needs of the wards are various. In some wards the pressing need may be better police protection -- in others, adequate sewage disposal -- in still others, housing or conservation or transportation.

The aldermen know intimately the needs of the people in their area. These people are their neighbors. So we find it natural that aldermen -- representing their constituents -- will be more concerned about some matters than others -- that they will resist change in some endeavors and will welcome changes in others.

This is also true of representative government in Congress and in the State legislature.

A natural consequence of this process is a slowing down of some governmental activity. In some instances the interests of all the people may be endangered or overlooked.

It has been charged that the city of Chicago has been slow in achieving some urgently needed improvements. If at times the council has been slow, it is because aldermen and community leaders have been striving to protect their people and their neighborhoods.

I believe in that principle. And in most cases what is good for the neighborhood is good for the city.

The city council, however, is the legislative branch of government for the entire city, and each alderman is duty bound to pass laws for the interest of all the people. The city -- not the ward -- must command first allegiance.

No individual or group -- no political party or political faction -- should have the right to block that which is good for all the city -- or to attempt to pass ordinances contrary to the interest of all Chicago.

I ran as a Democratic candidate for mayor of Chicago. I am proud to be a Democrat.

Tonight, however, as Mayor of Chicago -- I want to declare for all to hear -- that my employer is all the people of Chicago -- Democrats, Republicans, and Independents -- of every economic group, of every neighborhood and every community.

I have no intention of interfering in any way with the proper functions of the city council. But, as Mayor of Chicago, it is my duty to provide leadership for those measures which are essential to the interests of all the people -- and, if necessary, to exercise the power of veto against any measures which would be harmful to the people.

The City Council has under consideration measures which will improve and modernize city government. I refer to the proposals of the Home Rule Commission.

The council has affirmed the transfer of budget making to the Mayor's office and the creation of the office of Deputy Mayor.

I hope that the council will pass the recommendations of the commission which are now before it. These are bills that would relieve the council of administrative and technical duties. They would permit the aldermen to devote most of their time to legislation.

I urge the council to consider quickly other commission recommendations that will do much to modernize and make more efficient and representative our city government.

Many of the Home Rule recommendations would give added duties and responsibilities to the Mayor and his department heads. It must never be forgotten, however, that the city council as the legislative body has the ultimate authority over the city government. Just as I fully accept the duties and responsibilities of the executive office, so do I recognize the duties and responsibilities of the City Council.

In the recent intense and bitter campaign many of the issues raised were designed to confuse and mislead. Tonight, as I begin my four years as mayor, I ask nothing more of the people of Chicago and the City Council than to judge me by actions and accomplishments in the next fours years as the Chief Executive of this great city.

I want to express the appreciation and admiration which I know all the people of Chicago have for the administration of Martin Kennelly. He will always be remembered as a Mayor who made important contributions to his city.

Chicago can be thankful that under his administration and through the cooperation of the City Council much was accomplished. There are great projects under way -- slum clearance -- new housing -- school building -- superhighways -- street-lighting projects -- neighborhood redevelopment -- off-street parking in neighborhood communities -- and many other improvements. I shall not only support these projects, I shall speed them vigorously and with energy. I will permit nothing to stand in the way of Chicago's growing civic consciousness and civic integrity.

In the period before us, there are a great many things to do -- great problems to overcome.

During the war, and the difficult period of readjustment which followed it, the people of Chicago, and the nation, accepted the inevitable limitations and shortages. These conditions affected essential services, prevented much needed improvements and curtailed even normal maintenance.

We are all aware of the problems which have arisen -- problems that all cities have in common -- housing, police protection, human relations, juvenile delinquency, transportation and schools. Some of these problems have their roots in the years of war-time stress and post-war adjustment. Others are natural consequences of urban growth and population pressures.

We not only have to cope with our present needs, but to answer the growing demand by our citizens for new services. I do not believe that the purpose of government is to provide the vital services at their minimum. It isn't enough to dispose of garbage in such a way as to meet minimum health standards. It isn't enough to have a transportation system which barely meets minimum needs and operates at a loss.

We can't be satisfied with a school system in which 14 thousand students must attend double shift schools, and where classes are overcrowded and where school buildings are old and dilapidated.

We want the finest police and fire departments in the nation.

We must provide the opportunity for every citizen to have decent housing. We must have slum clearance. While we are clearing the slums, we must prevent the spread of blight into other neighborhoods.

These are immediate problems. These are the things that the people of Chicago want now.

There are long-range problems to consider also -- and we will initiate and encourage the development of programs and projects to meet them.

But we must not scatter our man power, our resources, or dissipate our time on what the city should have -- when there is so much that the city must have.

We must take first things first. We must concentrate our efforts on city services which are essential to keep the people of Chicago the healthiest, best protected and most prosperous in the nation.

These are the things that our people want now. These are the services which make a city strong and vigorous. They make our city a better place in which to live.

It would be difficult, and perhaps unwise, to say which of the programs of the city should be given priority.

But, underlying all our problems, and basic to all our programs, is the city's desperate need for additional revenue.

No one knows this better than the members of the city council.

We will strive to eliminate waste. We will economize and increase our efficiency. But no matter how successful we are in achieving these goals, we still will not be able to give minimum essential services unless the State legislature unlocks the handcuffs on our revenue power.

The members of the State legislature know full well what it takes to operate a city and that taxes on property cannot meet the costs of essential services of the second largest city in the nation.

In the past years, the city administration and city council have unceasingly sought additional revenue from the state, as well as new sources of non-property revenue to meet the continual rising cost of government.

Many proposals have been made to the state by the cities for additional revenue from the state as well as powers to raise non-property revenue. Thus far the state has given the cities very little relief.

In 1952, the Mayor's commission on revenue, which was not a political commission in any way, analyzed the needs of Chicago. This non-partisan commission estimated that for corporate purposes, the city needed immediately 23 million dollars in additional revenue.

The commission's recommendations for additional tax powers were presented to the legislature. The result was to make available not more than five and a half million of the 23 million dollars needed. The city was left helpless in the face of rising costs.

The legislature is now in session. We will present Chicago's needs for additional revenue from the state -- and for authority to obtain more non-property revenue to maintain and improve the city's services.

We will go to the legislature as often as necessary.

We are not asking for special privileges. We are asking for what we think we are justly and rightfully entitled to.

In this task -- as well as in meeting other basic problems of the city -- I shall urge the active cooperation and support from individuals, business, civic, and labor organizations and community groups.

This task can only be accomplished by teamwork, cooperation and unity. It is not a political problem but a civic problem. In the very near future, I shall call a meeting of representatives of all interests in Chicago to join with me and the city council in preparing an integrated legislative program to bring Chicago the things it vitally needs.

The program presented to the legislature will represent a program for Chicago. And the state must answer to the people of Chicago.

There are many problems before us that demand immediate attention and action.

There is no dispute among us that we need more police and a better police department -- that we need more schools and more teachers -- that government should be continuously streamlined and modernized -- that there must be something done to improve our transportation system -- and to get mass transportation off the streets.

We must eliminate the blight in middle-aged neighborhoods and utilize vacant and under-used areas of the city for the building of new homes and apartments.

A community betterment program will also include cleaner and safer street, extension of sewers, the expansion of street lighting and a bigger street-cleaning department, and a realistic human relations program. More recreational facilities, too, are needed in the neighborhoods, more playgrounds and parks to keep children and teenagers off the street and out of the juvenile home.

I am fully aware of the vital importance of the Mayor's appointing power. The status of thousands of civil service workers will be unaffected. We must have a program of continual improvement in civil service. We must have a program that will attract the best young men and women from our universities and communities into the service of the city.

There will be changes in the administrative policy-making positions. And I will appoint the best men and women available, regardless of political affiliations.

It has been my philosophy all my life that good government is good politics. It is this philosophy I will follow as Mayor of Chicago. Whatever political aspect there is in the mayor's office will be deferred while we concentrate on the immediate and urgent problems that face the city.

These are just some of the problems that must be met quickly -- these problems are the first order of business.

In meeting them we can draw a lesson from Chicago's inspiring history.

When Cook County was organized in 1831, Chicago -- then a tiny village in the great Prairie State -- became a seat of Justice. It became a town in 1833 and a city in 1837.

By that time Chicago was confident of its future. Its people saw tremendous possibilities in its location and in its natural facilities.

They had visions of Chicago as a great center of lake transportation. The State of Illinois began developing the Illinois and Michigan Canal, and the Federal Government helped in the development of the harbor.

Then came the growth of the railroads. The vision of Chicago as the hub of the transportation network of the nation came along.

These pioneers knew they were on the verge of a great expansion, and they drew strength and inspiration from their dream of a mighty Chicago.

We today are in a similar position. With the development of the St. Lawrence Seaway we can become the greatest inland port of the world.

We are the aviation crossroad of the continent, and we can be the world's aviation center.

We, too, can be pioneers, pioneers of a greater city of the future -- just as our forefathers were.

I have met too many people with a defeatist attitude toward our great city. They spoke gloomily of the great problems that would face the chief executive of the second largest city of the nation.

When I listened to these people, I felt that in many ways they were strangers to the real Chicago.

I mean the Chicago that is the great economic and financial giant of the midwest.

I mean the Chicago made up of contributions from people of every race, religion and nationality.

I mean the Chicago made up of fine neighborhoods.

I mean the Chicago made up of splendid churches and temples of every faith.

I mean Chicago -- the medical center of the world -- with the finest hospitals in the nation.

I mean Chicago with its great universities.

I mean the Chicago that has maintained the Art Institute -- the Museum of Natural History -- Libraries -- and other cultural institutions which are among the foremost in our land.

I mean the Chicago that is a city of parks and beaches.

I mean the railroad center of the nation and the air center and truck center of the continent.

I mean Chicago -- the hog butcher of the world -- the city of broad shoulders.

I mean Chicago that is destined to have the largest inland port in the world.

I mean Chicago, with an unlimited potential, to be the magnificent city of the future.

I mean the Chicago of "I WILL."

This is the real Chicago.

This is the reputation by which Chicago should be known to the people of the Nation and the World.

As Mayor I feel that one of my greatest responsibilities is to present a true picture of our great city -- and to erase the unreal notion that many people have of Chicago and its people.

The Mayor's office is no ivory tower. Its problems cannot be solved with a slide rule. There are no miracles -- there are no bargains in government as in anything else.

But if work, and sincerity, and the highest dedication to the city and its people can bring programs into reality --

If effort, intelligent approach and courage can solve problems --

If humility, patience, and vision can surmount obstacles -- then Chicago will go forward.

To this end I will dedicate myself -- to a sincere, honest and vigorous administration, to maintain the fabric of civil life in Chicago and lay a concrete foundation for a renewal of faith in our City's dignity and future.

With your cooperation and with cooperation of the people of Chicago, and with God's help, we shall not fail.

SHOOT TO KILL, SHOOT TO MAIM -- 1968

In April, 1968, in the wake of the assassination of Martin Luther King Jr., Chicago erupted into a major riot. An angry Mayor Daley turned to the subject of the riots at his press conference on April 15, 1968.

(Source: Chicago Sun-Times, April 16, 1968.)

1. Formed a nine-man committee to prepare "a careful and comprehensive analysis" of the disorders.
2. Rebuked Police Supt. James B. Conlisk, Jr. for failing to issue orders to shoot arsonists and looters.
3. Instructed Conlisk, in the future, to issue shoot-to-kill orders against arsonists and shoot-to-stop orders against looters.
4. Ordered his riot committee to investigate incidents of violence in Chicago schools following the murder of Dr. Martin Luther King, Jr.

Daley informed the press conference he had just told Conlisk "very emphatically and very definitely that an order be issued to shoot to kill any arsonist or anyone with a Molotov cocktail."

He also said orders should be issued to shoot, but not kill, "anyone looting any stores in our city."

Shortly before 6 p.m. Monday, Police Supt. Conlisk [issued the following orders above] his signature to all commanding officers:

1. Arson, attempted arson, burglary and attempted burglary are forceable felonies.
2. Such force as is necessary, including deadly force, shall be used to prevent the commission of these offenses and to prevent the escape of perpetrators.
3. The commanding officers will ensure that the above and General Order 67-14 are continually reviewed at all roll calls effective immediately and continuing through 22 April, 1968.

General Order 67-14 was issued by former Police Supt. Orlando W. Wilson last May, and spells out legal and department policy guidelines on the use of force likely to cause death or great bodily harm.

Daley ordered the committee to investigate the actions of the police and fire departments and the Illinois National Guard, and to examine the role and responsibilities of schools and communications media "in times of serious disorder."

The nine-member panel will be headed by U.S. District Court Judge Richard B. Austin.

The committee, expected to follow closely the procedures used by the Kerner commission in probing civil disorders, was ordered to complete its report in 90 days.

The committee likely will rely heavily on interviews with persons involved in the disorders and on data gathered from policemen, firemen, national guardsmen, fire victims, looters, public officials and eyewitnesses.

Other members are:

Franklin M. Kreml, president of the Chicago Police Board; Charles Siragusa, executive director of the Illinois Crime Investigating Commission; Daniel Walker, president of the Chicago Crime Commission; Justin Stanley, president of the Chicago Bar Assn.; William E. Peterson, president of the Cook County Bar Assn.; Thomas Mulroy, chairman of the Mayor's committee on Police and Community Relations; Maynard P. Venema, president of the Chicago Assn. of Commerce and Industry, and city Corporation Counsel Raymond F. Simon.

Speaking of police directives on use of weapons, the mayor said he was "very much disappointed to learn that every policeman pounding a beat was to use his own discretion."

They mayor added: "He (the policeman on the beat) should have had instructions to shoot arsonists and to shoot looters.

"In my opinion, there should have been orders to shoot arsonists to kill, and to shoot looters in order that they be detained."

"And in my opinion, MACE (a nonlethal chemical weapon) should have been used."

Orders School Inquiry

The mayor, announcing the formation of his investigation committee, ordered it to pay special attention to "the role and responsibility of the schools."

He said he had reports that, after the death of Dr. King, "there was the beating up of girls by fellow students, the slashing of teachers and extortion and payoffs" in the public school system.

Daley asserted: "Something has got to give. What kind of society are we building?

"We've got to face up to this question -- not with brutality and not with any cruel ideas, but with some kind of discipline.

"If we don't, we won't have any government."

Daley said he was surprised and disappointed to learn that, of almost 2,700 persons arrested during the disorders, "only 16 were arrested for arson."

He added, "Anyone who doesn't think there's a conspiracy ought to go take a look, and see which buildings have been spared."

Asked if current studies have determined that MACE is safe to use, the mayor said: "I don't know. I'm not a chemist. But it's a lot safer than having people burned to death."

'Arsonist A Murderer'

Asked if Conlisk was on his way out as police superintendent, Mayor Daley said, "I wouldn't want to discuss that at this time. I want to await the report of my committee."

Asked for clarification of his statement that he was "disappointed," the mayor said, "Yes, I was disappointed. There's no reason for this lawlessness and immorality. An arsonist is a murderer and should be shot right on the spot.

"The looters -- you wouldn't want to shoot the youngsters -- but you can shoot them in the leg and detain them."

Fire Comr. Robert J. Quinn, at his City Hall office, denied a report that he made the recommendation to Mayor Daley for sterner action against arsonists. He said:

"You had better talk to the mayor about this matter. This is a matter between the mayor and the police department. The mayor makes up his own mind. I did not make any recommendations about police action with regard to the disturbances.

"I had my hands full fighting fires."

Raps Robinson

Daley also condemned Cook County Public Aid Director William H. Robinson for statements he made during the disturbance.

The mayor made it clear that he regarded Robinson's statements to news gatherers as critical of the response of city officials to the rioting.

Daley said: "A certain county official said there weren't any city officials in the troubled areas. Call Mr. Robinson and maybe he can explain why the Lawndale office of the Public Aid Department closed down at 1 o'clock.

"It's easy to get up and criticize and condemn. But the city facilities were told to stay open.

"And they did remain open, offering food and shelter, 24 hours a day."

The mayor referred to 14 field offices of the Chicago Committee on Urban Opportunity (the city's anti-poverty agency).

'Arson Worst Crime'

During questioning by reporters, Daley repeatedly referred to what he saw as the failure of police to use stern action during the disturbance.

He said, "The crime of arson is to me the most hideous and worst crime."

Asked why a shoot-to-kill policy wasn't observed during the disturbances, the mayor said, "I assumed the orders were given. I would assume any (police) superintendent would issue orders to shoot any arsonists on sight."

The mayor said the newly formed committee will meet in the next two or three days and will report within 90 days.

"I'll surely take action to improve the police department," he said.

Daley also criticized radio and television coverage of the disturbances.

He said, "On the TV, they were putting every rumor on the air. It was the greatest example of hysteria since the stockyard fire (in 1934), when one radio man was on the air saying that the whole South side was on fire. And it was just the stockyards."

Duties of Committee

At the outset of his press conference shortly after noon, the mayor issued a statement announcing creation of the committee. . . .

THE WALKER REPORT - 1968

Chicago has been the scene of many types of riots. None has been more violent than the four days of fighting between Chicago Police and mobs of anti-Viet Nam war demonstrators at the National Democratic Convention held in the city during the summer of 1968. What follows is an excerpt from the official report of an investigating commission that was asked to examine the riot.

(Source: A Report Submitted by Daniel Walker, Director of the Chicago Study Team, to the National Commission on the Causes and Prevention of Violence, Chicago, and Washington, 1968.)

During the week of the Democratic National Convention, the Chicago police were the targets of mounting provocation by both word and act. It took the form of obscene epithets, and of rocks, sticks, bathroom tiles and even human feces hurled at police by demonstrators. Some of these acts had been planned; others were spontaneous or were themselves provoked by police action. Futhermore, the police had been put on edge by widely published threats of attempts to disrupt both the city and the Convention.

That was the nature of the provocation. The nature of the response was unrestrained and indiscriminate police violence on many occasions, particularly at night.

That violence was made all the more shocking by the fact that it was often inflicted upon persons who had broken no law, disobeyed no order, made no threat. These included peaceful demonstrators, onlookers, and large numbers of residents who were simply passing through, or happened to live in, the areas where confrontations were occurring.

Newsmen and photographers were singled out for assault, and their equipment deliberately damaged. Fundamental police training was ignored; and officers, when on the scene, were often unable to control their men. As one police officer put it: "What happened didn't have anything to do with police work."

The violence reached its culmination on Wednesday night.

A report prepared by an inspector from the Los Angeles Police Department, present as an official observer, while generally praising the police restraint he had observed in the parks during the week, said this about the events that night:

"There is no question but that many officers acted without restraint and exerted force beyond that necessary under the circumstances. The ledership at the point of conflict did little to prevent such conduct and the direct control of officers by first line supervisors was virtually non-existent."

He is referring to the police-crowd confrontation in front of the Conrad Hilton Hotel. Most Americans know about it, having seen the 17-minute sequence played and replayed on their television screens.

But most Americans do not know that the confrontation was followed by even more brutal incidents in the Loop side streets. Or that it had been preceded by comparable instances of indiscriminate police attacks on the North Side a few nights earlier when demonstrators were cleared from Lincoln Park and pushed into the streets and alleys of Old Town.

How did it start? With the emergence long before convention week of three factors which figured significantly in the outbreak of violence. These were: threats to the city; the city's response; and the conditioning of Chicago police to expect that violence against demonstrators, as against rioters, would be condoned by city officials.

The threats to the City were varied. Provocative and inflammatory statements, made in connection with activities planned for convention week, were published and widely disseminated. There were also intelligence reports from informants.

Some of this information was absurd, like the reported plan to contaminate the city's water supply with LSD. But some were serious; and both were strengthened by the authorities' lack of any mechanism for distinguishing one from the other.

The second factor -- the city's response -- matched, in numbers and logistics at least, the demonstrators' threats.

The city, fearful that the "leaders" would not be able to control their followers, attempted to discourage an inundation of demonstrators by not granting permits for marches and rallies and by making it quite clear that the "law" would be enforced.

Government -- federal, state and local -- moved to defend itself from the threats, both imaginary and real. The preparations were detailed and far ranging: from stationing firemen at each alarm box within a six block radius of the Amphitheatre to staging U.S. Army armored personnel carriers in Soldier Field under Secret Service control. Six thousand Regular Army troops in full field gear, equipped with rifles, flame throwers, and bazookas were airlifted to Chicago on Monday, August 26. About 6,000 Illinois National Guard troops had already been activated to assist the 12,000 member Chicago Police Force.

Of course, the Secret Service could never afford to ignore threats of assassination of Presidential candidates. Neither could the city, against the background of riots in 1967 and 1968, ignore the ever-present threat of ghetto riots, possibly sparked by large numbers of demonstrators, during convention week.

The third factor emerged in the city's position regarding the riots following the death of Dr. Martin Luther King and the April 27th peace march to the Civic Center in Chicago.

The police were generally credited with restraint in handling the first riots -- but Mayor Daley rebuked the Superintendent of Police. While it was later modified, his widely disseminated "shoot to kill arsonists and shoot to maim looters" order undoubtedly had an effect.

The effect on police became apparent several weeks later, when they attacked demonstrators, bystanders and media representatives at a Civic Center peace march. There were published criticisms -- but the city's response was to ignore the police violence. . . .

BIBLIOGRAPHY

Published material on the city of Chicago, while abundant, is frequently inaccessible. Local newspaper files, census reports, municipal records, and contemporary studies prepared by civic organizations or students concerned with some special phase of Chicago are the most obvious sources. In addition, there are a myriad of secondary works on the Windy City, some of which have been listed in the following selected bibliography. In a very real sense then, this bibliography is intended to act as a solid beginning for those students interested in pursuing the subject further.

Obviously, the best libraries housing the formidable collection of primary and secondary works on Chicago are to be found in the city of Chicago itself. However, much valuable research can be done at institutions in one's own place of residence, as most of the better libraries in the country include works concerned with Chicago in their own collections. Unfortunately, many of the works about Chicago are now out of print, and hard to obtain. The Municipal Reference Library in Chicago provides the interested students with a valuable collection of both public and private documents, as well as important secondary studies. In addition, there are literally hundreds of pages of unpublished material which are available at the Chicago Historical Society, and in the theses and dissertation rooms of the University of Chicago, and the University of Illinois.

Finally, then, the following titles have been chosen by the author as being most representative of the mass of works most readily available to those interested in working on the history and development of Chicago. It is hoped that they will be found useful in amplifying the picture of the city of Chicago which is presented in the foregoing pages.

BOOKS

Abbot, Edith. The Tenements of Chicago, 1908-1935. Chicago, 1936. Excellent documented study of this serious urban problem.

Abrahamson, Julia. A Neighborhood Finds Itself, New York, 1959.

Addams, Jane. Twenty Years at Hull House, New York, 1910. Very good autobiography of the great social worker and her achievements.

Andreas, Alfred T. History of Chicago, 3 vols. Chicago, 1884-86. Old but still a valuable study as far as it goes.

Andrews, Wayne, Battle For Chicago. New York, 1946.

Angle, Paul M., ed. The Great Chicago Fire, Described in Seven Letters by Men and Women Who Experienced its Horrors, and Now Published in Commemoration of the Seventy-Fifth Anniversary of the Catastrophe. Chicago, 1946.

Appleton, John B. The Iron and Steel Industry of the Calumet District. University of Illinois Studies in the Social Sciences. vol. 13, no. 2. Urbana, Illinois, 1925.

Arpee, Edward. Lake Forest Illinois: History and Reminiscences, 1861-1961. Lake Forest, Illinois, 1963.

Asbury, Herbert. Gem of the Prairie, An Informal History of the Chicago Underworld. New York, 1940. Interesting, colorful work. Often quite revealing.

Barton, Elmer. A Business Tour of Chicago, Depicting Fifty Years of Progress. Chicago, 1887.

Baruch, Hugo. Carrying a Gun for Al Capone; The Intimate Experiences of a Gangster in the Bodyguard of Al Capone. New York, 1932. Factual, frightening study of the heyday of Chicago gangsterism.

Biographical Sketches of the Leading Men of Chicago, Written by the Best Talent in the Northwest. Chicago, 1868. Though quite laudatory, an invaluable work on the early leaders of Chicago.

Birmingham, George A. From Dublin to Chicago: Some Notes on a Tour of America. New York, 1914.

Bishop, Glenn A., and Gilbert, Paul T. Chicago's Accomplishments and Leaders. Chicago, 1932. Contains much valuable information, but laudatory from start to finish.

Blanchard, Rufus. Discovery and Conquests of the North-West, with the History of Chicago. Wheaton, Illinois, 1880.

Bowen, Louise De Koven. Fighting to Make Chicago Safe For Children. Chicago, 1920. Interesting personal account by one of the leading Chicago reformers.

----------------------. Growing Up With A City. New York, 1926.

----------------------. The Public Dance Halls of Chicago. Chicago, 1917.

Breese, Gerald W. The Daytime Population of the Central Business District of Chicago. Chicago, 1949. Fascinating study of a subject not entirely unique to Chicago.

Bregstone, Philip P. Chicago and Its Jews. Chicago, 1933. Good ethnic study of Chicago's important Jewish element.

Bright, John. Hizzoner, Big Bill Thompson, New York, 1930. Colorful, humorous biography of one of Chicago's notorious mayors.

Bross, William. History of Chicago. Chicago, 1876.

Buder, Stanley. Pullman: An Experiment in Industrial Order and Community Planning, 1880-1930. New York, 1967. Scholarly, well documented work on the famous city established by George Pullman.

Burnham, Daniel H., and Kingery Robert. Planning the Region of Chicago. Chicago, 1956. Very good first-hand account of the work of the Chicago Planning Commission.

Burns, Walter N. The One Way Ride: The Red Trail of Chicago Gangland from Prohibition to Jake Lingle. New York, 1931.

Butt, Ernest. Chicago Then and Now. Chicago, 1933.

Campbell, Edna F., Smith, Fanny R., and Jones, Clarence F. Our City--Chicago. New York, 1930.

Chamberlain, Everett. Chicago and Its Suburbs. Chicago, 1874. Early study of an important urban development.

Chapin, Louella. Round About Chicago, Chicago, 1907.

Chatfield-Taylor, Hobart C. Chicago, Boston, 1917.

The Chicago and Interurban Trolley Guide. Chicago, 1907.

Chicago and Northwestern Railway Company. Yesterday and Today: A History. Chicago, 1905. Good study of the role played by this railroad in the development of Chicago and the West.

Chicago Area Transportation Study. Final Report. 3 vols. Chicago, 1959, 1960, 1962.

Chicago Association of Commerce, eds. Chicago, The Great Central Market, Chicago, 1923.

Chicago Board of Trade. Annual Report of the Trade and Commerce of Chicago. Chicago, 1858-90.

Chicago City Council Committee on Local Transportation. A Comprehensive Local Transportation Plan for the City of Chicago. Chicago, 1937.

Chicago Commission on Race Relations. The Negro in Chicago: A Study of Race Relations and a Race Riot. Chicago, 1922. One of the best studies on the Chicago race riot of 1919 by the official committee established to study its causes.

Chicago Evening Post. The Book of Chicago, 1911. Chicago, 1911.

Chicago Herald. Illustrated History of Chicago, Chicago, 1887.

Chicago Plan Commission. Forty-Four Cities in the City of Chicago. Chicago, 1942.

Chicago Plan Commission. Master Plan of Residential Land Use of Chicago. Chicago, 1943.

Chicago's First Half Century: The City as it was Fifty Years Ago and As It Is Today. Chicago, 1883.

City of Chicago Department of Development and Planning. The Comprehensive Plan of Chicago. Chicago, 1966.

Cleaver, Charles. Early Chicago Reminiscences. Chicago, 1882.

Colbert, Elias. Chicago: Historical and Statistical Sketch of the Garden City. Chicago, 1868.

Colbert, Elias, and Chamberlain, Everett. Chicago and the Great Conflagration. Chicago, 1871. Excellent first hand account of the great fire.

Condit, Carl W. The Rise of the Skyscraper. Chicago, 1952.

——————. The Chicago School of Architecture: A History of Commercial and Public Building in the Chicago Area, 1875-1925. Chicago, 1964. Very well done work, containing an excellent collection of photographs and illustrations.

Cook, Frederick F. Bygone Days in Chicago: Recollections of the "Garden City" of the Sixties. Chicago, 1910.

Coyne, F. E. In Reminiscence: Highlights of Men and Elements in the Life of Chicago. Chicago, 1941. Colorful study containing a number of interesting anecdotes.

Cromie, Robert. The Great Chicago Fire. New York, 1958. An up to date well documented work on the great tragedy.

Currey, Josiah S. Chicago: Its History and Its Builders: A Century of Marvelous Growth. Chicago, 1912.

Cutler, Irving. The Chicago-Milwaukee Corridor: A Graphic Study of Intermetropolitan Coalescence. Evanston, Illinois, 1965. Important work on the development of a megalopolis in this region.

David, Henry. The History of the Haymarket Affair, A Study in the

American Social-Revolutionary and Labor Movements. New York, 1936. Still the best work on the subject.

Davis, Allen F. Spearheads For Reform: The social Settlements and the Progressive Movement, 1890-1914, New York, 1967. Descriptive, detailed study of the founding and work of the various settlement houses in the nation with major emphasis on Chicago.

Davis, James L. The Elevated System and the Growth of Northern Chicago. Evanston, Illinois, 1965.

Dedmon, Emmett. Fabulous Chicago, New York, 1953. Very colorful popular history of the city.

Dennis, C.H. Victor Lawson: His Life and His Work, Chicago, 1935. Solid biography of the great Chicago millionaire.

Drake, St. Clair, and Cayton, Horace. Black Metropolis: A Study of Negro Life in a Northern City. New York, 1935. Penetrating study of life in the black ghetto of Chicago.

Drury, John. Old Chicago Houses. Chicago, 1941.

Duncan, Otis D., and Duncan, Beverly. The Negro Population of Chicago: A Study of Residential Succession. Chicago, 1957. Very scholarly, well documented work dealing with the growth and mobility of blacks in Chicago.

Elliot, James L. Red Stacks Over The Horizon: The Story of the Goodrich Steamboat Line, Grand Rapids, 1967.

Fiske, Horace S. Chicago in Picture and Poetry. Chicago, 1903. Although old, this work contains a valuable collection of artistic materials.

Frazier, E. Franklin. The Negro Family in Chicago. Chicago, 1932. Pioneering work in the sociology of the Chicago Negro.

Frynell, F.M. The Physiography of the Region of Chicago. Chicago, 1927. Solid geographical study of the region.

Gale, Edwin O. Reminiscences of Early Chicago and Vicinity. Chicago, 1902.

Gates, Paul. The Illinois-Central Railroad and Its Colonization Work. Cambridge, 1934. Detailed study of the influence of this railroad in the development of Chicago.

Gilbert, Frank. Centennial History of the City of Chicago; Its Men and Institutions, Chicago, 1905.

Gilbert, Paul T., and Bryson, Charles L. Chicago and Its Makers, Chicago, 1929. Popular history of the growth of the city.

Goode, J. Paul. The Geographic Background of Chicago. Chicago, 1926. Excellent, scholarly study of the natural factors and forces that helped to make Chicago a major urban center.

Goodspeed, Edgar J. History of the Great Fires in Chicago and the West. Chicago, 1871.

Gosnell, Harold F. Negro Politicians: The Rise of Negro Politics in Chicago. Chicago, 1935. Outstanding work on the development of political consciousness among the blacks of Chicago.

————————. Machine Politics: Chicago Model. Chicago, 1937. Excellent work on the operations of political parties in the city and Cook County.

Gottfried, Alex. Boss Cermak of Chicago. Seattle, 1962. Superior biography of the first Slavic Mayor of Chicago, as well as a detailed history of politics and government in the city.

Hamilton, Henry R. The Epic of Chicago. Chicago, 1932.

Hansen, Harry. The Chicago. New York, 1942. Detailed study of the Chicago River, its influence in the region, and importance in the growth of Chicago.

Harper, William H., ed. Chicago: A History and Forecast, Chicago, 1921.

Harrison, Carter H. Growing Up With Chicago. Chicago, 1944. Personal reminiscences of a Chicago mayor of the early twentieth century.

Hayes, Dorsha. Chicago, Crossroads of American Enterprise. New York, 1944. Good study of the business activity of Chicago and its vicinity.

Helvig, Magne. Chicago's External Truck Movements, Chicago, 1964.

Hoffman, Charles Fenno. A Winter in the West: Letters Descriptive of Chicago and Vicinity in 1833-34. Chicago, 1882.

Hoyt, Homer. One Hundred Years of Land Values in Chicago, 1830-1933. Chicago, 1933.

Hull House Residents. Hull House Maps and Papers. New York, 1895. Invaluable collection of records and documents of the first and most important Chicago settlement house.

Illinois Commission on Human Rights. Non-white Population Changes in Chicago's Suburbs. Chicago, 1962.

BIBLIOGRAPHY

Johnson, James D., compiler. A Century of Chicago Streetcars, 1858-1958, Wheaton, Illinois, 1964.

Jones, John H., and Britten, Fred A., eds. A Half Century of Chicago Building: A Practical Reference Guide. Chicago, 1910.

Kirkland, Joseph. The Story of Chicago. 3 vols. Chicago, 1892-94. Though old, this work contains a great deal of information concerning the early years in the growth of the city.

Kogan, Herman, and Wandt, Lloyd. Lords of the Levee: The Story of Bathhouse John and Hinky Dink. Indianapolis, 1943. Colorful, humorous account of two of the most famous ward bosses of Chicago.

----------------------------------. Chicago: A Pictorial History. New York, 1958. Well done work consisting of excellent illustrations, photographs and brief narrative.

Lepawsky, Albert. Home Rule For Metropolitan Chicago. Chicago, 1932.

Lewis, Lloyd, and Smith, Henry J. Chicago, the History of Its Reputation. New York, 1929. One of the best books on Chicago.

Lindsay, Almont. The Pullman Strike, The Story of a Unique Experiment and of a Great Labor Movement. Chicago, 1942. Very well done, scholarly study of the great strike of 1894.

McClure, James B., ed. Stories and Sketches of Chicago: An Interesting, Entertaining, and Instructive Sketch History of the Wonderful City "By the Sea." Chicago, 1880.

McIntosh, Arthur T. Chicago. Chicago, 1921. Popular history of the city, laden with anecdotal material.

Mason, Edward G., ed. Early Chicago and Illinois. Chicago, 1890.

Masters, Edgar Lee. The Tale of Chicago. New York, 1933. A brilliant, often sarcastic and critical portrait of the city by the great American poet.

Mayer, Harold M. Chicago: City of Decisions. Chicago, 1955. Excellent geographic study of the physical growth of the city.

----------------. The Port of Chicago and the St. Lawrence Seaway. Chicago, 1957. Very good study of the growth and development of the port, and the effects of the building of the seaway on the city of Chicago.

----------------. The Railway Pattern of Metropolitan Chicago. Chicago, 1943.

Mayer, Harold M., and Wade, Richard C. Chicago: Growth of a Metropolis. Chicago, 1969. Up to date, pictorial history of Chicago, accompanied by a clear, but brief, narrative.

Merriam, Charles, E. Chicago, A More Intimate View of Urban Politics. New York, 1929.

Mitchell, C.C. and Co. The New Chicago. Chicago, 1920. Good example of urban boosterism.

Moody, Walter D. Wacker's Manual of the Plan of Chicago: Municipal Economy. Chicago, 1911.

Moses, John, and Kirkland, Joseph. History of Chicago. 2 vols. Chicago, 1895.

Nelli, Humbert S. The Italians in Chicago, 1880-1930. New York, 1970. Brilliant study in ethnic mobility in the city.

Orear, George W. Commercial and Architectural Chicago. Chicago, 1887.

Palmer, Vivien M. Social Backgrounds of Chicago's Local Communities. Chicago, 1930. Very good study of the socio-cultural aspects of Chicago's different neighborhoods, but dated.

Pasley, Fred D. Al Capone: The Biography of a Self-Made Man. New York, 1930.

Pierce, Bessie L. As Others See Chicago: Impressions of Visitors, 1673-1933. Chicago, 1933. Excellent compilation of contemporary writings and views of the city.

----------------. A History of Chicago. 3 vols. New York, 1937-1957. This massive study is probably the best single work on the history of Chicago, but only carries the story up to the 1950's.

Plumbe, George E. Chicago, the Great Industrial and Commerical Center of the Mississippi Valley. Chicago, 1912. Very laudatory work, but contains valuable information.

Putnam, James W. The Illinois and Michigan Canal: A Study in Economic History. Chicago, 1918. Very valuable work on the canal, and its influence in the founding of Chicago.

Quaife, Milo M. Checagou: From Indian Wigwam to Modern City, 1673-1835. Chicago 1935. Scholarly work on the very early history of the region, and the earliest beginnings of the village of Chicago.

---------------. Chicago and the Old Northwest, 1673-1835: A Study of the Evolution of the Northwestern Frontier, together with a History of Fort Dearborn. Chicago, 1913.

----------------------. Chicago's Highways Old and New: From Indian Trails to Motor Road. Chicago, 1923.

Randall, Frank A. History of the Development of Building Construction in Chicago. Urbana, Illinois, 1949.

Reichman, John J., ed. Czechoslovaks in Chicago. Chicago, 1937.

Reminiscences of Chicago During the Civil War. Chicago, 1914.

Reminiscences of Chicago During the Forties and Fifties. Chicago, 1913.

Reminiscences of Early Chicago. Chicago, 1912.

Rossi, Peter H., and Dentler, Robert A. The Politics of Urban Renewal: The Chicago Findings. New York, 1961. Detailed, well documented study of urban renewal projects in the city.

Royko, Mike. Boss: Richard Daley of Chicago. New York, 1971. Bitter, extremely uncomplimentary short biography of the mayor of Chicago.

Salzman, David M. Waterway Industrial Sites, A Chicago Case Study. Chicago, 1966.

Schiavo, Giovanni E. The Italians in Chicago; A Study in Americanization. Chicago, 1928.

Schroeder, Douglas. The Issue of the Lakefront. An Historical Critical Survey. Chicago, 1963. Well documented, detailed study of the politics and issues surrounding the lakefront developments in the city.

Seeger, Eugene. Chicago, the Wonder City. Chicago, 1893. Good propaganda history for the city at the time.

Shackleton, Robert. The Book of Chicago. Philadelphia, 1920.

Siegel, Arthur, ed. Chicago's Famous Buildings. Chicago, 1965. Up to date architectural history of Chicago.

Sinclair, Upton. The Jungle. New York, 1906. Devastating muckracking classic of the Chicago meat packing industry.

Smith, Henry J. Chicago's Great Century, 1833-1933. Chicago, 1933. Excellent history of the city done in a scholarly fashion.

Solomon, Ezra, and Bilbija, Zarko G. Metropolitan Chicago: An Economic Analysis. Glencoe, Illinois, 1959.

Spear, Allan H. Black Chicago: The Making of a Negro Ghetto, 1890-1920. Chicago, 1967. Well written, documented study of the evolution of the black communities in the city. One of the best works on the subject.

Steadman, Robert F. Public Health Organization of the Chicago Region. Chicago, 1930.

Taaffe, Edward J. The Air Passenger Hinterland of Chicago. Chicago, 1952.

Thompson, William Hale. Chicago: Eight Years of Progress: January, 1923. Chicago, 1923. Interesting, but highly slanted view of the city written by one of its most famous and notorious mayors.

Thrasher, Frederick M. Chicago's Gangland. Chicago, 1923.

Tuttle, William Jr. Race Riot: Chicago in the Red Summer of 1919. New York, 1970. Brilliant, modern evaluation of the great Chicago race riot. Excellent history.

University of Chicago Center for Urban Studies. Mid-Chicago Economic Development Study. 3 vols. Chicago, 1966.

Vanderbosch, Amry. The Dutch Communities of Chicago. Chicago, 1927.

Waldrop, Frank. McCormick of Chicago. Englewood Cliffs, New Jersey, 1966. Excellent biography of the influential Chicago newspaper publisher.

Wirth, Louis. The Ghetto. Chicago, 1928. Pioneering work in the sociology of ghetto area residents.

Zorbaugh, Harvey W. The Gold Coast and the Slum. Chicago, 1929. Solid, scholarly study comparing two ways of life in the city of Chicago.

ARTICLES

"Airports: The King is Dead." Newsweek LX. July, 1962.

Atcheson, Richard. "Marina City: Chicago's Pies in the Sky." Holiday XXXVIII. December 1965.

Bach, Ira J. "Chicago Expands its Burnham Plan." The American City LXXVI. September, 1961.

Bennet, Edward H. "The Beginning of the Lake Front Improvement in Chicago." The American City XVI. March, 1917.

Bowen, William. "Chicago: They Didn't Have to Burn it Down after All." Fortune LXXI. January, 1965.

Bunch, R. J. "The Thompson-Negro Alliance." Opportunity VII. March, 1929.

"Chicago." The Architectural Forum CXVI. May, 1962.

"Chicago, 1856." Putnam's Monthly Magazine VII. June, 1856.

"Chicago." Holiday II. May, 1947.

"The Chicago Tribune." Fortune May 1934.

Crane, Jacob L. "Ultimately, the Regional City." The American City Magazine XXXIV. January 1926.

Dedman, Emmett. "Hustling Metropolis." Saturday Review of Literature XXXIV. December, 1951.

Dent, Newton. "The Romance of Chicago." Munsey's Magazine XXXVII. April 1907.

Fuller, Henry B. "Chicago's Book of Days." The Outlook XVI. October, 1901.

Gates, Alfred. "Chicago Unravelling Fiscal Snarl." National Municipal Review XXI. April, 1932.

Ginsburg, R. A. "Czechs in Politics." Czech and Slovak Leaders in Metropolitan Chicago, ed. Daniel D. Droba. Chicago, 1934.

Hallgren, Mauritz A. "Chicago Goes Tammany." The Nation CXXXII. April, 1931.

Hayes, A.A. "Metropolis of the Prairies." Harper's New Monthly Magazine LXI. June, 1880.

Head, Franklin H. "The Heart of Chicago." The New England Magazine VI. July, 1892.

Husband, Joseph. "Chicago: An Etching." The New Republic V. November, 1915.

Jones, Dallas L. "Chicago in 1833: Impressions of Three Britishers." Journal of the Illinois State Historical Society XLVII. 1954.

"The Kelly-Nash Machine." Fortune. August, 1936.

Kingsberry, J.B. "The Merit System in Chicago From 1915 to 1923." Public Personnel Studies IV. November, 1926.

Lee, Guy A. "Historical Importance of the Chicago Grain Elevator System." Agricultural History XI. January, 1937.

Lepawsky, Albert. "Chicago, Metropolis in the Making." National Municipal Review XXX. April, 1941.

Ligget, W. "The Plunger of Chicago." American Mercury XXV. March, 1933.

Masaryk, Alice G. "The Bohemians in Chicago." Charities XIII. December, 1904.

Masters, Edgar Lee. "Chicago: Yesterday, Today and Tomorrow." The Century Magazine XCIV. July, 1928.

Mayer, Harold R. "South Lawndale." Forty-Four Cities in the City of Chicago. Chicago, 1942.

Monroe, Lucy B. "Art in Chicago." The New England Magazine VI. June, 1892.

Morgan, William T.W. "The Pullman Experiment in Review." Journal of the American Institute of Planners XX. No. 1. 1954.

Nicholson, Meredith. "Chicago." Scribner's Magazine LXIII. February, 1918.

O'Keeffe, P.J. "The Chicago Stock Yards." The New England Magazine VI. May, 1892.

Parton, James. "Chicago." Atlantic Monthly XIX. March, 1867.

Robinson, George F. "The Negro in Politics in Chicago." Journal of Negro History XVII. April, 1932.

Runnion, Ray. "Chicago the Beautiful." The Nation CLXX. July, 1945.

Ryerson, Joseph. "What Chicago Looked Like a Century Ago." Townsfolk Magazine XXXIX. March, 1949.

Schiller, Andrew. "Chicago's Miracle: How a Unique Railroad Man Is Making Money Out of Commuters---And Makes Them Like It." Harper's Magazine CCXXXII. January, 1966.

Shedd, James. "Chicago: The Central Market." The World To-Day IX. September 1905.

Smith, Henry, J. "Chicago, Her Plans and Her Growing Pains." The Century Monthly Magazine XCI. March, 1927.

NAME INDEX

Adamowski, Ben, 56, 57
Addams, Jane, 26, 29, 33, 34, 35
Adler, Dankmar, 23
Altgeld, John P., 31
Armour, J. Ogden, 35
Armour, Philip D., 16, 30
Anson, A.C., 26

Balatka, Hans, 25
Ball, Charles B., 36
Beery, Wallace, 34
Berry, Edwin, 56
Bigelow, Liberty, 11
Blaine, Mrs. Emmons, 34
Boone, Levi D., 10
Bowen, Louise DeKoven, 38
Boyington, William W., 16
Bremer, Fredrika, 7
Browne, Charles F., 37
Browne, Francis F., 23
Buckingham, Clarence, 46
Buckingham, Kate, 46
Bull, Ole, 9
Burnham, Daniel, 23, 24, 28, 37
Bushman, Francis X., 34
Busse, Fred A., 36

Capone, Al, 44, 45, 46, 47, 48
Carelton, Henry Guy, 21
Cermak, Anton J., 48, 49, 50
Chappel, Eliza, 2
Chesbrough, Ellis S., 9, 19
Clark, Mark, 63
Clarkson, Ralph, 37
Cleveland, Grover, 31
Clybourne, Archibald, 1
Cobb, Henry Ives, 28
Colosimo, Jim, 43
Colvin, Henry D., 22
Conlisk, James, 60
Corning, Erastus, 6
Corwin, Tom, 6
Crerar, John, 26
Crosby, Uranus H., 15

Daley, Richard J., 54, 55, 57, 58, 59, 62, 64

Darrow, Clarence, 43, 44
Davis, Rennie, 62
Dawes, Rufus C., 44
Debs, Eugene V., 31
Dellinger, David, 62
Depoele, C.J. Van, 26
Dever, William, 44
Dewey, John, 32
Dippel, Andreas, 38
Donnelly, Michael, 35
Douglas, Paul H., 59, 60
Douglas, Stephen A., 9, 12, 13, 16
Dumphy, John M., 20
Dunne, Edward F., 34, 36, 43
Dunne, Finley Peter, 22
Durkin, Martin P., 54
Dyer, Thomas, 8
Dyhrenfurth, Julius, 7

Easley, Ralph M., 29
Edward VII, 13
Eisenhower, Dwight D., 54
Ellsworth, Elmer, 13
Emmerson, Louis L., 48
Evans, John, 7
Everleigh, Ada, 34
Everleigh, Minna, 34

Farnam, Henry, 9
Fergus, Robert, 4
Fermi, Enrico, 52
Field, Marshall, 23, 24, 29, 30, 36, 51
Fielden, Samuel F., 25
Franks, Robert, 44
Fuller, Henry, 11, 37

Gage, Lyman J., 29
Garden, Mary, 41
Garland, Hamlin, 37
Garrett, August, 5
Gary, Joseph E., 25
George V, King of England, 46
Gilmore, P.G., 17
Goldberg, Bertrand, 58
Goodrich, Grant, 7

Grant, Ulysses S., 17
Greeley, Horace, 6
Griffin, Walter Burley, 39
Gulini, Carlo Maria, 63

Haines, John C., 13
Hampton, Fred, 63
Hanrahan, Edward, 63
Harding, Warren G., 43
Harper, William Rainey, 29
Harrison, Carter H., 22, 23, 24, 28, 30
Harrison, Carter H., Jr., 32, 33, 34, 38
Harvey, George, 21
Hauser, Phillip M., 53
Heacock, Russell, E., 3
Healy, G.P.A., 7
Hearst, William Randolph, 33
Heath, Monroe, 22
Henderson, Charles R., 40
Hoffmann, Julius, 62, 63
Hood, Raymond, 44
Hopkins, John Patrick, 30
Hughes, John, 5
Hunt, Robert M., 28
Hutchins, Robert Maynard, 52

Insull, Samuel, 28, 45, 47
Isaaks, Abraham, 34

Jefferson, Joseph, 4
Jefferson, Mrs. Joseph, 4
Jenney, William LeBaron, 24, 26
Joffre, J., 40

Keller, Joseph G. 44
Kelley, Florence, 28
Kelly, Edward J., 50, 51, 52
Kennelly, Martin, 53, 54
King, Martin Luther, Jr., 59, 60
Kinzie, John H., 2
Kunstler, William, 63

Landis, Kennesaw M., 41
Lathrop, Julia, 29, 33, 36

Leopold, Nathan, 44
Lincoln, Abraham, 6, 11, 12, 13, 14, 15
Lingle, Jake, 48
Loeb, Richard, 44
Love, C.W., 43
Lunty, Orrington, 7

MacVeah, Franklin, 21
Mason, Roswell B., 19
McClellan, George B., 12
McCormick, Cyrus, 5
McCormick, Cyrus, Jr., 29
McCormick, Robert R., 35, 38
McDowell, Mary, 34
McKim, Charles, 28
McKinley, William, 34
Medill, Joseph, 20
Miltimore, Ira, 5
Monroe, Harriet, 38
Morris, Buckner S., 5
Mueller, Adolph, 6

Nitti, Frank, 49

O'Banion, Dion, 45
Ogden, William B., 3, 4, 5
O'Leary, Kate, 19
Olmstead, Frederick, L., 28

Palmer, Potter, 16
Palmer, Mrs. Potter, 29
Parmalee, Franklin, 10, 11
Parsons, Albert, 25
Patti, Adelina, 9, 26
Peck, Ferdinand Wythe, 26
Pinkerton, Allan, 7
Point du Sable, Jeane Baptiste, 1
Post, George B., 28
Pullman, George, 12, 14, 20, 24

Quarter, John, 5
Queen Elizabeth II, 57
Queen Victoria, 12

Reiner, Fritz, 54
Rice, John B., 5, 8, 15, 16

NAME INDEX

Rice, Wallace, 41
Riley, James Whitcomb, 21
Robbins, Raymond, 35
Rockefeller, John D., 27, 29
Roosevelt, Franklin D., 49, 50, 51
Rosenwald, Julius, 29, 31, 46
Root, George F., 14
Root, John W., 23, 24
Rutledge, Grady, K., 44

Seale, Bobby, 62
Sheffield, Joseph, 9
Shepherd, Robert H., 44
Sinclair, Upton, 36
Small, Albion W., 40
Smith, Alfred E., 44
Smith, Gypsy, 37, 38
Solti, George, 63
Spies, August, 25
Starr, Ellen Gates, 26
Stead, William T., 30
Stone, Melville E., 21
Storey, Wilbur F., 14
Stuart, William, 4
Sullivan, Louis, 23, 28, 33
Sweet, J.B., 14
Swift, Augustus, 21, 22

Taft, Lorado, 37
Taylor, Augustine Deodat, 1

Taylor, Graham, 29, 30, 36
Thomas, Theodore, 17, 28
Thomas, William I., 40
Thomason, Emory, 47
Thompson, James, 1
Thompson, Lydia, 18
Thompson, William Hale, 40, 42, 44, 46
Torio, Johnny, 43
Turpin, Ben, 34

Upton, George P., 11
Urban, Joseph, 50

Van Der Vaart, Harriet, 35
Van Osdel, John M., 8, 18, 21, 24

Wacker, Charles H., 37
Walker, Daniel, 62
Walker, Samuel J., 14
Warner, John, 60
Watkins, John, 1
Wentworth, John, 3, 11, 12, 13
Williamson, John Henry, 42
Wilson, Orlando, 57, 60
Wright, Frank Lloyd, 36, 39

Yerkes, Charles T., 23, 32

Zangara, Guisseppe, 50
Zueblin, Charles, 40
Zuta, Jake, 48